WORSHIP NOW
BOOK II

Worship Now
Book II

A Collection of
Services and Prayers
for Public Worship

Compiled by
Duncan B Forrester • David S M Hamilton
Alan Main • James A Whyte

THE SAINT ANDREW PRESS
EDINBURGH

First published in 1989 by
THE SAINT ANDREW PRESS
121 George Street, Edinburgh EH2 4YN
Copyright © The Saint Andrew Press 1989

ISBN 0 7152 0633 8

British Library Cataloguing in Publication Data

Worship Now.
Bk 2, A collection of services and prayers
for public worship
1. Christian church. Public worship—Rites
I. Forrester, Duncan B.
264

ISBN 0–7152–0633–8

The Publisher acknowledges financial assistance from
The Drummond Trust towards the publication
of this volume

This book is set in 12/13pt Baskerville
Typeset by J&L Composition Ltd, Filey, North Yorkshire
Printed in Great Britain by Bell and Bain, Glasgow

Contents

	Page
List of Contributors	vi
Introduction	vii
A Prayer for Advent	ix

Section I
Anthology of Prayers for Public Worship

(i)	*Prayers for the Opening of Worship*	5
(ii)	*Prayers of Adoration and Confession*	19
(iii)	*Prayers of Thanksgiving*	45
(iv)	*Prayers of Intercession*	51
(v)	*Closing Prayers*	65
(vi)	*Complete Prayers for Sunday Services*	69

Section II
Worship for the Seasons of the Christian Year

(i)	*Prayers for Advent*	89
(ii)	*Prayers for Christmas*	102
(iii)	*Prayers for Lent and Easter*	110
(iv)	*Prayers for Pentecost*	125

Section III
Sacraments and other Ordinances

(i)	*Prayers for Baptism*	135
(ii)	*Prayers for Communion*	145
(iii)	*Prayers for Marriages*	165
(iv)	*Prayers for Funerals*	174

Section IV
Acts of Worship for Special Services

(i)	*Affirmation of Faith and Commitment*	183
(ii)	*Prayers for Occasional Services*	191
(iii)	*Prayers for Peace, Justice and Healing*	211
(iv)	*Prayers for Informal, Small Group and Family Worship*	223

List of Contributors

BARBOUR, R A S, Dean of the Chapel Royal; former Moderator of the General Assembly. (RASB)

BROWN, Robert F, Queen's Cross Church, Aberdeen. (RFB)

CAMPBELL, Keith, St Aidan's Church, Broughty Ferry. (KC)

CRAWFORD, Michael S M, St Mary's Church, Aberdeen. (MSMC)

DOIG, Andrew B, former Moderator of the General Assembly. (ABD)

DRAKE, Wendy F, St Martin's Church, Edinburgh. (WFD)

FORRESTER, Duncan, Professor of Christian Ethics and Practical Theology, New College, Edinburgh. (DF)

GALLOWAY, Kathryn and Ian, former Joint Wardens of Iona Abbey. (KG and IG)

GORDON, Tom, Viewforth Church, Edinburgh. (TG)

GRAHAM, David, Rutherford Church, Aberdeen. (DG)

HARRIS, Stewart, former Deputy City Architect, Edinburgh. (SH)

JONES, Edmund, Irvington, New York. (EJ)

KESTING, Sheilagh M, St Andrew's High Church, Musselburgh. (SMK)

LEWIS, Alan, Professor of Constructive Theology, Austin Presbyterian Theological Seminary, Texas; formerly of New College, Edinburgh. (AL)

LONGMUIR, T Graeme, Chaplain, Strathallan School. (TGL)

McDONALD, Alan, Holburn Central Church, Aberdeen. (AM)

McDONALD, W J G, Mayfield Church, Edinburgh. (WJGM)

McIVER, N, Newhills Church, Aberdeen. (NM)

McLELLAN, A R C, St Andrew's and St George's Church, Edinburgh. (ARCM)

MATHESON, James, former Moderator of the General Assembly. (JM)

OGSTON, David, St John's Church, Perth. (DO)

REID, Alan A S, Chaplain, Aberdeen University. (AASR)

REID, David T, Cleish Church, by Kinross. (DTR)

SHAW, D W D, Professor of Divinity, University of St Andrews. (DWDS)

WINNING, Ann, Morvern Church, Lochaber. (AW)

WYLIE, W Andrew, Chaplain to the Offshore Oil Industry. (WAW)

Introduction

Worship Now, first published in 1972, was reprinted in 1976. It is now out of print. Although many have expressed regret at this, the original editors and The Saint Andrew Press felt that after the passage of years what was needed was a new book rather than a re-publication of the old. Of the original editors only one (Professor Whyte) was available to work on the new volume. The present editorial panel consists of the Revd Professor Duncan Forrester, Edinburgh, the Revd David S M Hamilton, Glasgow, the Revd Professor Alan Main, Aberdeen, and the Very Revd Professor James Whyte, St Andrews.

Our aim is not to provide an alternative to the more official service books and publications on worship, but to complement them. Nor do we aim to lay down some new norm for contemporary worship, but rather to open up new possibilities by showing the varied work of some of those who are seeking a contemporary idiom in worship. The material is meant to be seen as flexible and adaptable. Not all of it will be appropriate to everyone in the different settings in which we worship. But all that is published here has been used and is in use, and none of it has been specially written for this publication. We hope that the book may be seen as a resource, and that it will encourage others to 'conceive their own prayers'. It may be that some of the material stimulated by this book will find its way into our hands for inclusion in a future volume, and we will be very happy if it does.

'An unofficial book does not require to have the balance and careful composition expected of an official Book of Common Order.' So said the editors of the first volume. We have tried not to be too unbalanced, but we have found, as our predecessors did, that we are limited by what our contributors choose to send us. Thus we had hoped to have much more material for informal worship in small groups and small rural parishes, but not a great deal of such material has been submitted. It may be that the very nature of informal worship is that it must allow for spontaneity and is not written down. Similarly, our covering of the Christian Year is fragmentary. Because of the nature of the book, and the limitations of size, we have not felt obliged to cover everything. On the other hand, we have had more material than we can use for some sections, and already have the beginnings of a further volume, which we hope may follow.

We are most grateful to all those who sent (often with a modest disclaimer) material for our consideration. In some cases we have had to limit the amount selected simply for reasons of space. Where we have edited, we hope that the contributors do not feel that we have marred the text. We have not sought to impose liturgical or theological uniformity, but we have aimed at consistency in usage. In this, as in the whole enterprise, we acknowledge the unfailing help of The Saint Andrew Press.

Note: In the service orders, introductory notes and rubrics are italicised; responses (by individuals or by the congregation) are IN CAPITALS.

James A Whyte
Edinburgh, 1989

A Prayer for Advent

Thou God of compassion,
   whose heart is the heart of Jesus our brother,
   whose love enfolds all thy children;

Let our waiting be a waiting
   in hope and peace,
   for no one is lost to thee.

Let us fear not to offer thee
   our sorrow with our praise,
   for thou hast made our pain thine own.

Let us find joy in holy memories
   and give thee thanks,
   for they promise the joy of thy kingdom.

Let us bring freely before thee
   our shadows and regrets,
   for thou dost forgive and heal.

Let us wait with a quiet heart
   for him to whom all are dear,
   for he has made his home with us.

Let us trust that he will come
   to make us one with all the saints,
   for his Spirit is with us.

All praise to thee, our Father,
   to thy Son, Jesus Christ, our Lord,
   to the Spirit who dwells in our hearts,
   both now and for ever.   Amen.

James A Whyte

Section I

Anthology of Prayers for Public Worship

(i)   *Prayers for the Opening of Worship*   *Page*

1	W J G McDonald	'The heavens are telling...'	5
2	W J G McDonald	'Lord, this we believe...'	6
3	W J G McDonald	*'Worship the Lord...'*	7
4	Longmuir	'Mighty God...'	8
5	Longmuir	'Glorious God...'	9
6	Lewis	*'Whatsoever things...'*	10
7	Jones	'O God, our God...'	11
8	Jones	'Now comes the winter...'	12
9	Jones	'The night stars...'	13
10	A A S Reid	*'O Lord, I stretch forth my hands...'*	14
11	A A S Reid	*'After he had come down...'*	15
12	Doig	'Lord God Almighty...'	17
13	Doig	'Almighty and Eternal God...'	17

(ii)   *Prayers of Adoration and Confession*

14	Longmuir	'Almighty God, so wise and powerful...'	19
15	Longmuir	'Lord God Almighty...'	20
16	Longmuir	'Lord God, we praise you...'	21
17	W J G McDonald	'Loving God, generous Father...'	22
18	W J G McDonald	'The heavens declare your glory...'	23
19	McLellan	'O God, the light of the minds...'	24
20	McLellan	*'The Son of man did not come...'*	25
21	Kesting	'The Body is one...'	26
22	Kesting	'Sing a new song...'	28
23	Kesting	'Praise be to God the Father...'	29
24	Harris	'God is light...'	31
25	Galloway	'We believe, O God...'	32
26	Doig	'Almighty and ever gracious God...'	33
27	Doig	'Gracious God, our Father...'	35
28	Graham	'Stop at the crossroads...'	36
29	Crawford	*'A Prayer of Thanksgiving...'*	38

1

30 A A S Reid   'Eternal Father, whom the heavens...' 39
31 A A S Reid   'Almighty God, our true and
                          constant Father...'   41
32 Kesting   'We confess, Lord God, what we
                          are...'   43
33 Brown   'Those who live on the level of the
                          spirit...'   44

(iii)   *Prayers of Thanksgiving*

34 Longmuir   'Father, it is right...'   45
35 McLellan   'O Jesus Christ...'   46
36 Galloway   'Mysterious and loving God...'   47
37 Kesting   'God our Father, we thank you...'   48
38 Brown   'Gracious and eternal God...'   49

(iv)   *Prayers of Intercession*

39 Doig   'Almighty God, gracious Father...'   51
40 W J G McDonald   'Accept, O God, the gifts of our
                          hands...'   52
41 W J G McDonald   'We pray for people...'   54
42 McLellan   'The harvest of the Spirit...'   54
43 McLellan   'The Church's one foundation...'   56
44 Kesting   'God of the still, small voice...'   57
45 Kesting   'Lord God, in this time of worship...' 58
46 D T Reid   'Father in heaven...'   60
47 Shaw   'O Lord our God...'   61
48 Longmuir   'Lord, you are to be found...'   62
49 Longmuir   'Father, we pray...'   63
50 Longmuir   'Lord Jesus Christ...'   64

(v)   *Closing Prayers*

51 D T Reid   'Lord of creation...'   65
52 W J G McDonald   'Lord, the world is made by your
                          hand...'   66
53 Doig   (a) Dedication of Offerings   66
                        (b) Dedication of Offerings   67
54 Longmuir   'Father, may your world...'   67
55 Longmuir   'Like your disciples...'   67
56 Galloway   Closing Responses   68

(vi) *Complete Prayers for Sunday Services*

57 Brown	'Come, let us return to the Lord...'	69
58 Longmuir	'Eternal God...'	73
59 McIver	Prayers for use in Morning and Evening Worship	76
60 Matheson	A service devised as a guide for those called on to lead worship in the absence of a minister	78
61 Drake	Prayers for an ordinary Sunday Service	82

Anthology of Prayers for Public Worship

(i) Prayers for the Opening of Worship

1

The heavens are telling the glory of God.
>Bless the Lord, O my soul.
>Praise the Lord, all his people.
From our hearts, O God, we bless you for the day
>newly begun:
>>for sleep behind us, food within us, light upon us,
>>love around us,
>>for the needs and hopes that we have in common
>>with all people—and for all we hold in
>>common with the Church of Christ
>>throughout the earth.
Give us openness today:
>to one another in love;
>to you our God in response to your love for us.
>Give us honesty with ourselves.
Give us light, O Lord, give us cleanness of heart and
>thought.
Give us that inner balance and purpose and
>commitment which are nothing else than the
>peace of God.
Renew in us life and let the fruit of the Spirit be seen
>in us; that your good work in the world be
>done through us.
Above all, O God, show us the face of Jesus Christ.
>Set Him before us as Lord and King.

Grant that to be his disciples may be the great aim
    and desire of our hearts.
For his love's sake.

(W J G M)

2

Lord, this we believe:
    that in a world where there are kings and queens,
        and presidents and emperors, and
        governments and parties...
    you ultimately are the King.
Lord, this we believe:
    that in a world where there are parents and
        leaders, and teachers and advisers and
        personalities...
    you above all are Father to us.
Lord, this we believe:
    that in a world where there are so many people
        offering to help; so many people who make
        things difficult;
    where there are so many people making demands
        upon us; and asking help from us;
    where there are so many people...
    you are our helper and our strength.
Lord this we believe:
    that in a world that has power to destroy itself,
    in a world where there is enough food but not
        enough concern,
    enough fuel but not enough self-discipline;
    enough knowledge but not enough love—
    you are the one who can give meaning to our lives,
        and purpose and a future for all mankind.
Each of us is known to you:

what we have done and what we should do, and
    what we could be.
Forgive the many things that we have done wrong.
Help us to live as your sons and daughters, to
    know Jesus Christ, and to follow him all the
    way.

(W J G M)

3

Worship the Lord in the beauty of holiness.

Father, this is our worship—
    to turn away from the daily duties and the passing
        show,
    and from the work that awaits us tomorrow;
    to stand in the presence of what is real,
    to bow in the presence of the Eternal.
Father, this is our worship—
    to come running,
    to tell out before we forget it all that has befallen us,
    what we have done and achieved and enjoyed;
    to share it with one who knows it all and
        understands it all.
Father, this is our worship—
    to unburden our hearts of the things that we are
        ashamed of;
    things done and thought and said;
    things left undone too;
    to admit to what others would be surprised to
        know and shocked to know
    —and the desperate unbelief that takes possession
        of us and makes mock of our securities and of
        our pretensions.

For with you alone in forgiveness,
you alone can show us who you are and what our
lives are for.
Father, this is our worship—
to give expression to our hopes and desires,
that others might find amusing or pathetic;
the inmost aspirations and goals that we still hold
before ourselves
—not for fantasising but for true fulfilment.
Father, this is our worship—
not to speak too much;
to listen more than we usually do;
to reflect; to accept; and to resolve.
Father, this is our worship—
to see Jesus;
to be touched by him;
to come to our feet and rise up and follow him.
Father, this is our worship—we offer it to you.

(W J G M)

4

Mighty God, you are Father of a great family,
a family made up of people from every age,
drawn from the four winds and from every
continent and island.
Your community transcends time and space:
beings still unknown to us, yet known to you,
bright beings of superior powers, and human
beings blessed with hope
join in your great service.
Within your family each has a place in your love and
no one is neglected or overlooked.
Your care extends to every member

and every member plays a part in your
  perpetual praise.
Earthly and unearthly music blend,
nature and grace combine,
earth and heaven agree,
within the bright orbit of your shining.
May we, with all your saints on earth,
  now sing your praises in concert with
    the saints in heaven;
through Jesus Christ our Lord.

(T G L)

5

Glorious God, before whom mountains salute with
mist-capped peaks, rivers run their cascading courses,
lochs pulsate with silent ripples, trees of the field clap
their hands, and rolling hills cry aloud for joy; your
glory shines through tinted colour, breezes through
leaf-filled woods, sparkles in the rushing stream, and
wakens shores from peaceful slumbers. As we acknowledge you to be the Lord, let your light shine brightly
through the window of our hearts; let your presence
inspire our worship, your Spirit intensify our praise,
and the great company of the hosts of heaven join with
us in giving glory to you, Father, Son and Holy Spirit,
God, for ever and ever.

(T G L)

6

Whatsoever things are true, whatsoever things are honest, whatsoever things are just, whatsoever things are pure, whatsoever things are lovely, whatsoever things are of good report: if there be any virtue and if there be any praise, think on these things. Let us pray:

Almighty God, beyond all knowing, seeing, touching,
    and far transcending all our understanding,
    we hear in wondering suprise, in fear and
      trembling, and yet in freedom,
    your call to us to approach and meet you in your
      holy presence.
Your thoughts are not our thoughts, nor are your ways
    our ways;
    yet you invite and enable us to know your way and
      to think about your truth.
You dwell in light inaccessible, hid from our eyes;
    yet in every corner of the universe, in earth and
      sky and sea,
    you make your beauty and your grandeur plain
      for all to see,
    and in your Son you have revealed yourself in
      your great majesty and love.
    Seeing Him, we have seen the Father also;
    and we have heard the promise that those who
      now can only dimly see as in a mirror, shall in
      the end see and know you face to face.
And therefore this morning,
    although you are unutterable, ineffable, beyond
      describing or defining,
    we bring you our tiny thoughts, our flawed
      conceptions, and our feeble words.
In prayer and praise and proclamation
    we dare to speak about you and speak to you.
    Not by any power of ours to raise ourselves to you,

but by your lowly willingness to expose yourself to
    us,
we believe that here we touch the intangible,
here   detect   the   inaudible,   here   know   the
    unknowable.
Give us in our worship, the amazed excitement
of those who stand at the intersection of two
    worlds,
where transcendence meets the ordinary, eternity
    the temporal,
where healing encounters sickness, transfiguration
    ugliness, justice wickedness,
where   redemption   smothers   desperation   and
    comfort embraces grief and loneliness.
All of which may only happen by your Spirit, in whom
    we pray;
and   through   your   Son,   who   taught   us   to   say
    together: *Our Father....*

                                   (A L)

7

O God, our God, who has fathered us in the rejoicings
of heaven and mothered us with affections from the
womb of time itself, as you made known your own love
through a family in joyous Bethlehem and even more
in the larger family at tragic Golgotha, so we
remember your love and lean on it in moments of
celebration and moments of sadness or suffering.

    We bless you that we are not left alone—but by
grace and a spacious mercy brought into the extended
family of faith, into the bridal church which is the
Mother of us all.

    Teach us to live as children of hope and as the

time passes ever more to be renewed in the children as our hope—for your Promise was not just to us but to generations yet unborn, as numerous as the sand on the seashore.

O God, let not one of your family be forgotten or lost—make the family complete in its caring for the sick and the lonely, the dispossessed and the defected.

Open our hearts and keep open our doors—that none be counted as of nought. Open our hearts and keep open our doors that the King of Glory may come in.

This our prayer we offer through Jesus Christ our Lord.

(E J)

8

Now comes the winter and the night is nailed to the sky with hard bright stars—and the morning comes as white gladness and a day of familiar tasks.

Now comes the winter and with it still the fidelity of the God who keeps his people through good times and bad, through days of summer and hours of dread.

Now comes the winter and buried as seed the springtime of the soul and the promise of new life and the wing of the Spirit. Now comes the winter and we know what it is to be lonely and feel blue—and the weeping and rejoicing in our cities—and the suffering that wounds us all. Now comes the winter and with it the Lord of the winter. Now comes the winter and all is well.

So come to us gracious God with a holiness like unto the driven snow: come to us with a truth that divides the falsehood: but gracious Lord come to us

with the gentleness of the snowdrop and the vulnerability of a child whose Star we have seen in the East.

Come as the pardon in our folly—as the peace in
our distraction—and as the power in our helplessness.

This our prayer we offer through Jesus Christ,
our Lord.

(E J)

9

The night stars bore silent witness and called the
      Easter Dawn to sing:
    The canticles of wind and trees burst into glad
      praise in the garden:
    Bread broken at eventide opened eyes that were
      holden.
So hearts that were burdened and lives that were
      bereft and regrets that were heavy knew again
      healing for brokenness, and beloved Presence
      for empty loss—knew again mercy for failure,
      and hope for despair, and courage for fear.
Thus it was on the first Easter, O Lord.
    Thus let it be for us again, Lord—new beginnings,
      new ways, a new spirit, new life.
    Let the dream sing inside us.
    Let words, holy words, great words, words of cross
      and grace and tomb, words of long ago:
    let these words of the soul cast a spell upon us and
      make us a new people of a new age.
Forgive our unbelief—the small treacheries, the trivial
      goals, the shabby compromises, the vacant
      shadows.
    And let our souls, troubled by things that do not
      matter and satisfied with things that do not

satisfy, find new life, life in his Spirit, your
life.
O Saviour Christ, born in the tomb, be born in us—
and pray in us the prayers of peace for the
remembered past, the prayers of trust for the
baffling present, and the prayers of hope for
the unknown future.
This our prayer for your Kingdom's sake.

(E J)

10

*O Lord, I stretch forth my hands unto thee. My soul thirsteth
for thee as in a thirsty land. Cause me to know thy loving
kindness in the morning, for in thee do I trust. Cause me to
know the way wherein I should walk, for I lift up my soul
unto thee.*

O Lord our Father, whose Word is always such a new
thing that lazy and shallow mortals cannot grasp its
revolutionary power, we ask—as this Service begins—
for gifts of the Spirit to listen and respond so that we
may be changed in our souls.
　　If it is possible for a person, young or old, by
meditation and prayer to see a new direction that life
might take, then, Lord, may we now be able to pray.
For our ways are evil, and our hearts are shamefully
double, and we bear no fruit.
　　If there is a power in the reading and preaching
of the Scriptures that can cleanse the vision of the
doubtful, and sensitise the conscience of the hardened,
may that power be with us now.
　　If there is a mercy which can overreach the
perpetual and flagrant repetition of the sins that wreck

all life's goodness, may that mercy descend on each person here that asks for it.

And if it is possible for courage, and hope, and spiritual commitment to begin again in those who have forfeited these experiences, may we, O Lord, become by thy power more nearly the people we could and should be.

Sometimes, Lord, we doubt whether these things are possible.

Jesus said: All things are possible to those who believe.

Therefore we make our prayer in Christ's name.

(A A S R)

11

After he had come down from the hill he was followed by a great crowd. And now a leper approached him, bowed low, and said: Sir, if only you will, you can make me clean. Jesus stretched out his hand, touched him, and said: I will; be clean again.

Our Loving Father and Holy God, it is good for us to be here. For to this strong and ancient house have come people down the years, waiting in the quietness so that they might be encountered and shriven and directed by your unchanging holiness and unavoidable compassion. For we know that here is a word for our heart, a lamp for our feet, and a light for our path to lead us in the way everlasting. You have given us Christ, and we have met him on our way and personal journey; and he has come to offer us his broken body again and again for our healing. We would turn our lives towards the influence of his spirit and his teaching again.

Lord, when we leave this place may we indeed be able to say 'How lovely is thy dwelling-place'—not for anything the outward eye can see, but because we know that we have been led back to simple, fine and fundamental things again, and we know that you have given yourself to us in word and truth, O holy God, our refuge and our strength.

Father, we do not know each other's hearts; but you know all of us and each of us and we believe that nothing can ever separate us from that knowledge of yours which is love. You know our heights and depths, our hopes and fears. You know our private longings and secret dreams; you know our deep and terrible contradictions. You know what we would achieve in days to come; you know how poorly we have served you in days gone by. And so we offer all these things to you for guidance, for forgiveness and for healing. We claim over all our sins the power that is in the Cross. We claim over all our defeats and betrayals the promise of the empty tomb, and the hope of that new day which can begin for each of us, raising us from the dead. And because our greatest need is always for cleansing, we ask that, like the leper, we may do this simple thing—approach Jesus in our heart and say, Sir, if you will, you can make me clean; and may hear his reply to us: Indeed I will; be clean again.

So, Lord, we ask that your love may freely burn in us, so that our earthly passions turn to dust and ashes in its heat consuming; and that our worship may truly celebrate your being and your glory, through the re-consecration of each new life in this place.

I was glad when they said unto me: Let us go into the house of the Lord. Our feet shall stand within thy gates, O Jerusalem.

(A A S R)

12

Lord God Almighty, give to us, we pray, quietness of spirit, humility of mind and eager expectation of goodness as we draw near to you.

Lord, we rejoice in all that you are and all that you have made. Praise the Lord, O my soul and forget not all his benefits.

Eternal God, you dwell in light inaccessible, yet in Christ we behold you. Your wisdom passes thought in the magnitude of your purposes, yet our hearts can worship and our minds and hands can handle with reverence all that you have made.

Almighty Father, you wield power beyond our control, yet we need not fear. You guide the planets in their courses, yet you hold each one of us in love and for safety in the hollow of your hand—in childhood, manhood, age and death, to keep us still your own.

Loving Father, forgive us when we have doubted ... failed ... rebelled ... misused your gifts ... been unresponsive to your call.

Make this a day of new beginnings for us.

Show us your glory that all else may seem as dross.

Speak to us your word that all else may fall silent.

Give us of your Spirit that we may be cleansed
    and renewed and recommissioned for service
    through Jesus Christ our Lord.

(A B D)

13

Almighty and Eternal God, the God and Father of our Lord Jesus Christ, it is into your world we would come, and in your presence we would abide,

—into the world of your creative power and
genius and the experience of your Fatherly
care
—where power is never destructive and causes
none to fear
—where love is complete and so utterly
undeserved
—where the call is always intimately personal, so
that none of us can evade the challenge and
none of us feel left out of the promises.

Gracious God, walk freely in love in our world, the
personal world we know and the larger world in which
we are set,
—where lives are broken and divisions are
terrifying and fear of man and of the
unknown prevails
—where so many feel lost and alone and
unwanted
—where to receive seems reckoned always more
important than to give
—where the present has so little of permanence in it.

Forgive us, Lord, that we hesitate so often between
these worlds,
—knowing yearnings yet so easily satisfied with
material things
—having visions of good, yet so slow to be
obedient in a daring and adventurous way
—recognising deep needs but too selfish to put
ourselves at risk or cost that these may be met
—knowing all is not well with us, but reluctant to
expose ourselves to the full searching scrutiny
and radical renewal of the Christ of Calvary.

In this hour of worship, set us again in the joyousness
of your world where we belong, and grant us to find

purpose in living and peace in abiding, through
Jesus Christ, in whose name and words we pray:
Our Father....

(A B D)

(ii)   **Prayers of Adoration and Confession**

14

Almighty God, so wise and powerful that none can
stand against you, we praise you. You are stronger
than earthquakes, storms and raging seas: open our
eyes to an awareness of your power. You know the
secrets of the atom and the vastness of outer space:
open our minds to your wisdom and creativity. Your
love is so deep that you know the innermost secrets of
all your children: open our hearts to you as friend.

Powerful and loving God, you bring all things
under your rule. All monarchs and presidents, all
ministers and officers owe their allegiance to you. So
we ask to see your glory, a glory shown supremely in
your Son to whom you gave all authority, and a glory
which can be reflected in the lives of all whom Jesus
calls.

Lord God, you are our strength and our salvation.
We proclaim and adore your glorious name; through
Jesus Christ our Lord,
Let us confess our sins to God.
Lord God, we confess our lack of faith, especially
when we've doubted your power to achieve your
purposes. We confess our ignorance and our un-
willingness to learn more about you and more about
ourselves and others. We confess our sense of lone-

liness and failure: our feeling that there is no one who can help us with our problems. So, too, in silence, we remember this past week, the hurtful things said to others: the hurtful things done to others as well as ourselves. . . .

We confess to God Almighty and to the whole company of earth and heaven that we have sinned in thought, and word and deed, and through what we have left undone.

Lord, have mercy upon us:
CHRIST, HAVE MERCY UPON US: LORD HAVE MERCY UPON US.

May the Almighty and merciful Father have mercy upon you; pardon and deliver you from all your sins and give you time to amend your lives:
Through Jesus Christ our Lord.

(T G L)

15

Lord God Almighty, we praise you that in ancient times you declared your truth to the world through Israel; and when many of your people were faithless you raised up a remnant and spoke through fearless prophets.

Join us to the prophets of Israel and all the faithful unknown who have lived in faithless times; that with them we may praise your name as we ought. Above all we praise you for your Son Jesus Christ, who was not afraid to stand alone, and through whom we are born into the Israel of God. Lord, God Almighty, through the prophetic influence of the Holy Spirit we worship you in the name of Jesus Christ our Lord.

Let us confess our sins to God.

God of truth, we confess that we've been unwilling to stand up for your truth; we've refused to listen to the voices of the prophets in our own day—we confess, too, that your Church has been narrow-minded and intolerant, refusing to hear your voice in any institution except itself: and, in the silence, we confess that, separately and collectively, we have sinned in thought, word and deed, and in what we have left undone.

Lord have mercy upon us:

CHRIST, HAVE MERCY UPON US: LORD, HAVE MERCY UPON US.

God the Father, God the Son and God the Holy Spirit have mercy upon you, pardon and set you free from your sins, and give you time to change your lives:

Through Jesus Christ our Lord.

(T G L)

16

Lord God, we praise you
> because in you is life and joy and love.
We worship you
> because your life is always new and you sustain us
>> by your vitality.
We love you
> because you always care but never stifle.
We depend on you;
> and we remember your goodness to us and to
>> those who've gone before us.

We tell your story in every generation: you are our familiar God, God of Abraham, Isaac and Jacob, God and Father of our Lord Jesus Christ, God of a pilgrim people, your Church. We give all praise and glory to you, the God who loves us, through Jesus Christ who saves us, and who raises us to a new life of fellowship in his spirit.

Let us confess our sins to God.

Lord God, your Son Jesus Christ is the true vine and we are the branches. But we confess that we've become separated from you

by wilfulness—when we seek our own satisfaction;

by forgetfulness—when we neglect the true reason for gathering in this building;

by aimlessness—when we're carried along by life's routines;

by self-centredness—when we look inward at our own needs and problems, but do not look outward on what is true, wonderful and loving...so, too, in the silence we remember that we have sinned in thought and word and deed as well as in the things we've left undone:

Lord have mercy upon us:

CHRIST, HAVE MERCY UPON US: LORD, HAVE MERCY UPON US.

God the Father, God the Son and God the Holy Spirit have mercy upon you, pardon and deliver you from all your sins and give you time to amend your lives:

Through Jesus Christ our Lord.

(T G L)

17

Loving God, generous Father, omnipotent Lord; from the richness and the distractions of our world we come to you...to share with you our fears, our joys, our frailties, our tiredness, our hopes and expectations, our thanksgivings.

From being at other times strong and mature and
competent, we come to admit to you our
weakness.

From being at other times forgotten and of little
account in the world, we come to you to
rejoice in our value, we believe, in your sight.

From failure and sin and faithlessness we come to
be made clean and new again.

From being on our own we come to share in our
oneness with one another in your sight.

As disobedient children, as rebellious sons and
daughters, as disloyal subjects, as creatures who have
much to discover about the purpose of our being here,
we come for wisdom and direction; for clarity of
vision, where so much is obscure; for grace to bow
before the presence of the mystery where so much
seems so obvious...so that we may be free to weep,
and to laugh, and to sing, and to live....

So we come, O God.

(W J G M)

18

The heavens declare your glory, O God, and our
voices would not be silent. Not casually would we offer
praise, but full-bloodedly. Not as of duty or routine
would we ascribe glory and honour to you, our Father,
but from the depth of our being, from the living depth
of our hearts.

Not conventionally would we confess sin committed; duty undone; penitence and regret unexperienced;
joy and sorrow unexplored; sacrifice for Christ's sake
not accepted; pain not absorbed for the suffering of
the world.

Lord, break the shell of our conventional piety, and of our routine worship. Come to us in love, that we may not flinch from your love's embrace, nor decline your forgiveness, nor be deaf to your calling of us once again.

Lord, we have no original sins to confess, but only such as have tarnished the lives and weakened the witness of so many others before us. But we know that unless we confess, even the things that we are ashamed to confess, we cannot be forgiven; that unless we are reconciled to our neighbour and to one another we cannot be reconciled to you. So hear the sins that now silently we name: hear the names of those with whom we intend to be reconciled....

We do this in the name of Jesus Christ, our Lord.

(W J G M)

19

O God, the light of the minds that know you, the joy of the hearts that love you and the strength of the wills that serve you; grant us so to know you that we may truly love you, and so to love you that we may truly serve you, whom to serve is perfect freedom.

O God, the hearts which we bring to your worship are not hearts of love and praise: we are people with hearts of stone: cold with no warmth, hard with no tenderness, dead with no life. Take away our hearts of stone and give us new hearts, hearts of flesh and spirit and love. Take away our hearts of stone as we confess our sins, saying: ·

Eternal God, our judge and redeemer,
    we confess that we have tried to hide from you,

for we have done wrong.
We have lived for ourselves,
    and turned from our neighbours.
We have refused to hear the troubles of others.
We have ignored the pain of the world,
    and passed by the hungry, the poor, and the
    oppressed.

O God,
in your great mercy forgive our sin and free us
    from selfishness,
that we may choose your will and obey your
    commandments;
through Jesus Christ our Saviour.

It stands written: 'If God is for us, who is against
us? Neither death nor life, nor things present nor
things to come, nor anything else in all creation, shall
be able to separate us from the love of God which is in
Christ Jesus our Lord'. In Jesus Christ we are forgiven.

(A R C M)

20

*The Son of man did not come to be served but to serve
and to give up his life as a ransom for many.*

Lord Jesus Christ, you came to serve.
    As you came to a blind man and gave him sight
        come to us in our darkness and show us the
        things we cannot see.
    As you came to a man tormented in his mind
        and gave him peace and healing come to us in
        our tensions and make us whole.

As you came to Lazarus dead and brought him
from the grave,
come to us in our deadness and bring us to
real life now with our living Lord.

Lord Jesus Christ, you came not to be served but to
serve:
But we see life the other way round;
to get where we do not give,
to exploit whom we have not helped,
to use what we have not earned.
As you came to a dying thief and promised him
paradise,
come to us now in forgiveness and hope.

Lord Jesus Christ, you came to serve.
As you came to a friendless tax-gatherer
and gave him purpose and delight,
come to us and renew us with your high calling
that we may love and serve you, now and for
ever.

(A R C M)

21

*'The Body is one and has many members. If one member
suffers, all suffer together, if one member is honoured, all
rejoice together'* (I Corinthians 12:12, 26).

Lord God, we come together in worship to praise your
goodness and honour your carefulness.
As Creator, we are overwhelmed by you:
by the sheer size and beauty of the universe,
by the awful fury of earthquake, wind and fire,

by our smallness in the whole order of it all.

As forgiving and loving Father, we are surprised by
     you:

by the way you care for each specific detail of creation,

by the persistence with which you come to share our
     life,

to bear the burden of pain and loneliness,

to rejoice with us in each new opportunity given to us.

Lord God, as one who demands obedience, we wonder
     at you.

We cannot understand your sense of justice.

You do not turn away, as we would do, from those who
     disown you.

You do not always regard faithfulness with comfort
     and peace, as we would expect of you.

Still we ask, as of old:

Why do the wicked prosper?

Lord, your symbol is a cross, and we do not always
     understand.

Forgive us our faithlessness.

Still we look for revenge for past sins.

Still we turn aside from those who have hurt us.

Still we despise those who think differently from us.

We are arrogant in our faith.

We believe we are right and others are always wrong.

We are always ready to judge and condemn with a self-
     righteous conviction.

Lord, you have given us the power to bring unity or
     division into our lives.

You have blessed us with a variety of gifts which we
     can choose to guard or to share.

May we be found using our energy to build up and
     restore relationships that have been broken.

May we work for unity in diversity

so that we may find common ground on which to meet

all people for the sake of Jesus Christ our
Lord.

(S M K)

22

Sing a new song to the Lord!
Sing to the Lord, all the world!
Sing to the Lord, and praise him!
Proclaim every day the good news
that he has saved us.
Proclaim his glory to the nations,
his mighty acts to the people.

God our Father, praise be to you
for your love in Jesus Christ,
the love which restores and heals,
which forever presents your people with new
beginnings,
new songs to sing, new opportunities for service.

Praise be to you Lord Jesus Christ,
for your charge to Peter who,
though he denied you three times,
was to be your pastor in the new believing community,
restored and forgiven by you in the days after your
resurrection.

Praise be to you, Lord God, who in the power of your
Holy Spirit
creates, sustains and renews the Church,
presenting through it to the world,
a new vision,
new possibilities of healing the wounds of history,

new avenues of peace to explore.

O God, we come to you in all our mixed-up ways.
We confess we come to sing old songs,
to go over old words.
　　　Often we are conscious of a dullness of spirit, a
hopelessness, an inability to keep up with a world
which seems to move so fast. How can we sing a new
song when our thoughts are in the past? How can we
seize the opportunities for witnessing to your will when
we continue to deny you in fear of what the world
might say?
　　　And yet, Lord, we do love you—
　　　or else we would not be here.
We are conscious of our weakness and wish to be
　　　　　strengthened in our faith.
We are confused by so much of life and long to find
　　　　　the answers.
Forgive us our unfaithfulness
our shallow grasp of your love for us.
Let your risen glory shine in us with new brightness
that we may care more deeply and speak of our faith
　　　　　more confidently.
Give us grace to love what you command
and to desire what you promise
that in all the changes and chances of the world
our hearts may reflect your lasting joy of the world
through Jesus Christ our Lord.

(S M K)

23

Praise be to God the Father,
loving Creator of all things

whose purpose is that all should willingly live in
    communion with him and with each other.
God, our Father, we praise you for your patience and
    forgiveness,
your willingness to create anew through your
    compassion and love.
We praise you for your Son in whom you are brought
    so near to us and in whom we learn to see you
    as you are.

Praise be to God the Son,
suffering man in the midst of time
whose mission was to show the Father
and to let us experience forgiveness and love.
Lord Jesus Christ, we praise you for your
unbending obedience
your unceasing care in the midst of the struggles of
    humankind
your ever more urgent message of the coming
    Kingdom of God.
We praise you for your promised gift of the Holy
    Spirit
in whom the Church is formed and by whom it is
    inspired and encouraged

Praise be to God the Holy Spirit,
creating unity between people
whose purpose is to gather all into communion with
    the Father.
Holy Spirit, the Comforter, we praise you for the gift
    of insight,
the way you can open our closed eyes and soften our
    hardened hearts so that we may know God
    and our fellow human beings.
We praise you for your power to strengthen the
    Church as it is sent out into the world with the
    Gospel of peace for all.

Holy Trinity, forgive us when we fail to worship you as
    we ought,
when our lives fall short of true witness to you.
In the power of the Spirit, lift us up to see Jesus as our
    true friend and brother who brings us with
    him into the presence of the Father where he
    reigns in glory forever.

                           (S M K)

24

God is light: in him there is no darkness at all:
Only the man who loves his brother lives in the light.

Father,
you make the light shine out of darkness,
you make the sun rise on bad and good alike,
you give us Christ, the world's light:
we wake our minds to think of you.
You live in light beyond all thought,
yet through Christ our Lord we know you,
present here, in love and power:
we lift our hearts to praise you.

What is man, that you should remember him?
Or mortal man, that you should care for him?
Yet through our Lord Jesus Christ we know you care,
in him you come, not to judge us, but to forgive and
    set us free:
we know that it is enough for us
to face ourselves in your presence, as honestly as we
    can,
remembering—
how we have not cared,

how we have been too much wrapped up in ourselves,
too hard on others, too quick to blame;
how we have grumbled, when we should have been
thankful,
have criticised, when we should have tried to help;
how we forget the rest of the world, so long as we're all
right ourselves:
Lord Jesus, real light of the world,
help us to admit such things now, in your presence.

Lord, help us to accept forgiveness from you, and
from others:
take away our pride,
open our eyes to your glory,
help us to live in its light:
and may each of us help and strengthen the other, that
together we may come to know and love and follow
our Lord Jesus, in whose words we pray together: *Our
Father* ....

(S H)

25

We believe, O God, that you are the eternal God of
life.
We believe, O God, that you are the eternal God of
love.
We believe, O God, of all the peoples, that you have
created us from dust and ashes.
O God, who brought us to the joyous light of this day
Bring us to the guiding light of eternity.

God of life—our life. The life that flows through us
like the sea ebbing and surging, sometimes calm and

tranquil, clear and clean and full of promise. But sometimes turbulent, violent and dark and full of fear. God of life, you are there in all of life. We give you thanks for the breath within us, for the pain of life, for you are there also.

God of love—our love. The love of others for us, and our love for them, real even in the midst of unreality. And that love only the little expression of your great love, creating, redeeming, transforming, love that was hung on a cross. Look at Jesus—real love, love in the flesh, and all for us, and for all of us.

Now we remember that we are dust and ashes. Now we remember the times of despair, the feelings of uselessness, the bitterness of failure. Now we remember the rage within us, the cowardice within us, the cruelty within us. And how it hurts—it hurts us, it hurts other people, it hurts you. God, without you, we are lost, dead to change, imprisoned in dead sins, dead ways. We are dust and ashes. Recreate us, remind us now of how you made us.

LORD HAVE MERCY UPON US...CHRIST HAVE MERCY UPON US.

Listen...for God speaks in Jesus, saying, 'Your sins are forgiven. You are set free. Go in peace, come and follow me.'

Now you make us new people, human people, people of the spirit, people of the way. You have touched us, and we are yours, to live and love, to serve you and praise you. God, we believe. Help our unbelief.

(K G and I G)

26

Almighty and ever gracious God, it is good for us to be here, in the place where others have sought and found you, where we ourselves have asked of the Lord and found peace. We are come now, gladly, expectantly, thankfully, linking our prayers with the promise of *your Word*.

The Word says, 'The earth is the Lord's and the fulness thereof.'

Lord we are come, conscious of abundant provision for our needs in things material and in the deeper needs of the spirit, eager to bless the hand that guided and the heart that planned.

For skills of heart and hand, for food and shelter, for the way prepared for us by others, often at cost of sacrifice. For Christ in the midst, unchanged and unchanging, ceaselessly willing to work all things together for good, in the majesty of his love in the grace of his Cross, in the power of his Resurrection:

Praise the Lord, O my soul and forget not all his benefits.

The Word says, 'Except the Lord build the house, they labour in vain that build it'.

Lord we are conscious of our own inadequacy, so often ashamed and sorry where we have hurt by word or failed in action; hasty when we should have taken thought; silent when we should have been great hearts for truth or communicators of compassion; trusting too easily the counsels of men, too seldom seeking a word from the Lord; skilled in the use of the materials of time and so faltering in the fashioning of what will last in human relationships and abundant living.

Lord, hear our cry. Forgive us our sins and enter in that the structures of our life may be on your design, grounded on your truth and love and bearing the marks of your gracious presence.

Jesus said, 'The world will make you suffer. Be brave. I have defeated the world'.

Lord we are weak and fearful of the forces we cannot contain, in ourselves and in the world around us. Give us courage to go forward, knowing ourselves and our loved ones in the larger setting of your power and the deeper understanding of your love and the promised possession of your peace, through Jesus Christ in whose name and very words we pray: *Our Father....*

(A B D)

27

Gracious God, our Father, we thank you for so much,
    given so richly to enjoy.
      —the splendour of dawn and the glory of sunset
        and the comforting cover of the dark
      —the surging life of a city and the peace that falls
        by hillside or seashore.
We thank you for every gracious human relationship,
      —the enrichment of family ties
      —the creative growths of friendships
      —the discipline of work
      —and the liberty of leisure.
We thank you for all that leads us beyond this present
    world
      —for prayer, meeting with you, asking of you,
        listening to you
      —for the heritage of faith in the life of your
        Church, keeping us mindful of your truth
        and love
      —for immortal longings in our hearts and sudden
        glimpses of eternity in the midst of time.
As you bless us in the ecstasies of life, so draw near to
    us when we face our failures.
Gracious God, forgive us
      —for living selfishly, as if no one mattered but
      ourselves

—for living carelessly as if we belonged to
     ourselves
—for acting too quickly and thinking too late
—for unwise and unkind words, for cowardly or
     discourteous silence
—for being so ready with our criticisms and so
     scant with our sympathies
In such a moment of self-awareness, of bitter
regret or wistful longing we thank you that all of life is
understood and transformed in the presence and
power of Jesus Christ, your son and our Lord.

Lord grant us that presence, grant us that power,
Through Jesus Christ.

(A B D)

28

This prayer is based on Jeremiah 6:16.

Stop at the crossroads, look down the ancient paths,
     ask yourself,
which is the way that God comes down?

Lord God
You have brought us here by many roads...
Down old closes:
     Sunday Schools: where once we heard the story of
          your patient love and kindest purpose
     homes where we agreed to parent's persuasion
     ancient churches with historic traditions
     Sabbath days when we were feeling bad and
          needing good.
Through newer streets:
     responding to a neighbour's hurried invitation

understanding the need for a baby to be given a
> name

finding a conscience

seeking reality

moving with the rhythm of a popular hymn tune

hearing rumours that Jesus was drawing the
> crowds again...

from highest blocks and lowest basements

from all the ups and downs of life together

from knowledge and from ignorance

from crevasses of despair, along thin ledges of
> anxiety

from stony faces or smiling fields, elated or cast
> down

rising to glorify.

LORD WE CONFESS THAT ALL OF US HAVE STUMBLED

We have been uncertain of the road

ashamed to ask directions after so long a time
> away

disorganised ourselves, we have been a barrier to
> others

lacking the vision to see ahead, we have blinded
> others by our prejudice

BUT NOW OUR ROADS HAVE REACHED YOUR HOUSE

—a meeting point of word and world...

HELP US NOW

to look down the ancient path your Word has
> travelled

to see it come to us

not just as lines of black marks on the white pages
> of an old book

but as a living lighting message passed down the
> road to us from time's beginning

once shouted by crowds

now carried by a thin and lonely voice

once a gift of old men, and then again the
> discovery of children

once hidden in the mountain's mist
then bill boarded for all to read
on a sign post cross where all our roads
    converge...
WHICH IS THE ROAD THAT GOD COMES DOWN?
WHERE IS THE WAY THAT GOD GOES ON?
For the love of your Son, our friend Jesus Christ.

(D G)

29

A Prayer of Thanksgiving, Confession, and Supplication with direct quotes from J B Phillips, The New Testament in Modern English.

Thanks be to God—the blessed controller of all things, the King over all kings, the Master over all masters and the one who lives in unapproachable light. (I Timothy)
    We are glad, Father that you in your infinite wisdom have given us not a spirit of fear, but a spirit of power, love, and a sound mind. (2 Timothy)
    We give thanks for the tremendous generosity of grace and kindness that you, Father, have expressed towards us in Christ Jesus. (Ephesians)
    We give thanks, Almighty God, that in your Son you have given us a full and complete expression of yourself. (Colossians)
    FATHER—FORGIVE US OUR SINS.
    So often we maintain a façade of 'religion'—but our very conduct denies its validity. (2 Timothy)
    Instead of being open and receptive to the stranger in our midst, we have been like wells without a drop of water in them. (2 Peter)

Father, we admit to our ignorance and insensitiveness almost as if we live blindfold in a world of illusion. (Ephesians)

FATHER, FORGIVE US.

Almighty Father, help us to maintain a firm position in the faith and not allow ourselves to be shifted away from the living hope of the gospel. (Colossians)

Help us, Good Lord, to plant our feet firmly within the freedom which Jesus Christ has won for us—the freedom to serve one another in love. (Galatians)

You, Father in Christ, have done the utmost from your side, may we for that very reason, do the utmost from our side. (2 Peter)

And help us to see that your Kingdom is not a matter of a spate of words, it is the power of Christian living. (I Corinthians)

FATHER, WE ASK THIS IN YOUR SON'S NAME.

(M S M C)

30

Eternal Father, whom the heavens cannot contain, far less this house built with hands; whom our language in its frailty strains after, catching only hints and traces of your Being; we worship you in thankfulness and joy in the morning of this new day. The light of the sun has not failed us; the constant miraculous laws of the universe still hold us in being through their wonderfully intricate web of workmanship; and we have been sustained in health and strength by your Providence to come to this place at this hour, so that our souls might be set in you again as a nail is set in a sure place.

As children when they grow to manhood and womanhood, begin to understand in some fragmentary way what their parents may have done for them from birth, so do we—but with far greater obligation—begin to perceive, Father, what you have done for us all the days of our life.

We give thanks that you have made your purpose and your love for us known in Jesus Christ. We listen to the apostle's word and know it for truth: that in him was life, and the life was the light of men. And we ask that, receiving him, we may have the power again to become the children of God. We give thanks for this new opportunity in worship to turn from our selfish ways and hear this word about Jesus again, for our spirits are barren and thin from exposure to much worldliness. We praise you, Father, that nothing has diminished the extraordinary authority and spiritual truth of Christ's teaching, though human ages and revolutions have come and gone. We acknowledge the power of God coming through his life and words, moving still with uninhibited freedom through our darkened world, piercing the veneer of our social and personal life, confronting us again and again for decisions about matters of life and death. We acknowledge that we find him alive and speaking through people who do care for others; in men and women who do believe against the evidence; in young folk and older folk who do seem to be walking the way of the Cross in this world, asking for no recognition or reward, sharing strangely in the Resurrection by the colour and quality of their life.

Father, it sometimes seems incomprehensible—when we reflect on all your goodness—that we continue to live at the level we do. We confess our poverty of gratitude and awareness, our pride and shallow self-sufficiency, our fragility of will and lack of love. We have been indulgent with ourselves, and sharply critical of others, and we come for healing.

Almighty God, we confess that we have sinned in thought, word and deed, and in what we have omitted to do. Have mercy upon us, forgive us all our sins, confirm and strengthen us in all goodness and bring us to life everlasting, through Jesus Christ our Lord.

(A A S R)

31

Almighty God, our true and constant Father, receive our worship from this place and this time, in the Communion of the whole body of Christ. Your thoughts are not our thoughts, nor are your ways our ways. In our tiny creatureliness we cannot fail to recognise how high the heaven is above the earth, how distant east from west, how far your glory and majesty are from our temporary and myopic existence. But we know, Father, in our pitiful ignorance, that you have flung a bridge across these unspeakable distances, and that the bridge is Love. We could not come to you; but you have come to us in the broken, disguised and disgraced form that Love takes in our world, in the figure of Jesus—placarded outside the city wall for our sins, offering himself in place of the arrogant and the evasive, the clever and the calculating; taking on himself the pain of disavowal and public betrayal by those who once gave him their commitment. Father, we acknowledge that that language and that signature makes its way through to us most compellingly today. We cannot but understand it, though in the world's reckoning it is nonsense and scandal; it pierces our careful defences and disarms our easy composure, and speaks to our sufferings and contradictions as Word of Life.

So, Father we praise you for the Love new every morning; and for the Spirit, taking the things of Christ, even now, and making them fresh to our hearts. We praise you for the whole created universe in all its brilliant complexity and groaning travail as the place where your Word is to be spoken, and lived, and recognised. We praise you for the uncanny challenge of the Gospel by which we will be addressed again today; and for the hope of redemption and new life which it holds out to us and all the broken brothers and sisters of the Son of Man. Lord, give us today the hearing ear, and the discerning spirit.

Father, hear our confessions. We have deliberately wandered away into a solitude so fearful and heedless that we do not even recognise how lost we are, or how near the precipice is to us. We have gone after the voice of strangers, and closed with pleasures which do not satisfy. We have lived with a selfishness and an indifference which should disqualify us forever from the Christian fellowship and the community of the caring. And we need the cleansing of forgiveness as the parched ground needs the great rain.

Bring forth the best robe and put it on him. Bring forth a ring for his finger and shoes for his feet, and let us have a feast to celebrate this day. For this my son was dead, and is alive again; he was lost, and is found.

I was glad when they said unto me: Let us go into the house of the Lord. Our feet shall stand within thy gates, O Jerusalem.

(A A S R)

32

We confess, Lord God, what we are:
>we are not the people we like others to think we
>>are;
>we are afraid to admit even to ourselves what lies
>>in the depths of our souls.
But we do not want to hide our true selves from you.
We believe that you know us as we are, and yet you
>love us.
Help us not to shrink from self-knowledge;
>teach us to respect ourselves for your sake;
>give us the courage to put our trust in your
>>guiding power.

We also confess to you, Lord, the unrest of the world,
>to which we contribute and in which we share.
Forgive us that so many of us are indifferent to the
>needs of our fellow men and women.
Forgive our reliance on weapons of terror,
>our discrimination against people of different
>>races
>and our preoccupation with material standards.
And forgive us as Christians for being so unsure of our
>Good News and for being so unready to tell it.

Raise us out of the paralysis of guilt into the freedom
>and energy of forgiven people.
And for those who through long habit find forgiveness
>hard to accept,
>we ask you to break their bondage and set them
>>free.
Through Jesus Christ our Lord.

(S M K)

33

This prayer is to be used responsively.

Leader: Those who live on the level of the spirit have minds controlled by what the spirit wants and that brings life and peace.

All: IF THE SPIRIT OF HIM WHO RAISED JESUS FROM THE DEAD DWELLS WITHIN US, THEN THE GOD WHO RAISED JESUS CHRIST FROM THE DEAD WILL ALSO GIVE NEW LIFE TO OUR MORTAL BODIES THROUGH HIS INDWELLING SPIRIT.

Leader: The spirit we have received is not a spirit of slavery leading us back into a life of fear.

All: IT IS A SPIRIT THAT MAKES US SONS, ENABLING US TO CRY 'ABBA! FATHER!'

Leader: Gracious and ever-seeking God, to have life and peace and be free from fear; to believe we are 'sons' (and daughters) who can call you 'Father'; to know that the glory that awaits us far exceeds our suffering; to trust that the hope of that future will keep us joyful; to experience your love as the 'ever-fixed mark'—this is your gift to us through your spirit dwelling within us.

All: YOURS IS THE PRAISE AND THE GLORY THROUGH JESUS CHRIST OUR LORD.

Leader: To be able to speak and act for you in the world; to witness to your love and your truth in our everyday living; to stand for the things of the faith in this day of small things; to be instruments of your peace at our work and in our homes; to continue the ministry of Jesus, doing things greater even than he; to be ambassadors for Christ to reconcile and to heal—this is your purpose for us through your spirit dwelling within us.

All: YOURS IS THE PRAISE AND THE GLORY,
          THROUGH JESUS CHRIST OUR LORD.
Leader: Drive out the selfishness and the fear that cut
          us off from you and our neighbour, so that
          you are no longer crowded out of our lives.
All: GIVE US THE GIFT OF NEW LIFE THROUGH
          THE INDWELLING OF YOUR SPIRIT, THAT WE
          MAY ACHIEVE YOUR PURPOSE FOR OUR LIVES;
          THROUGH JESUS CHRIST, OUR LORD, AMEN.

(R F B)

(iii) **Prayers of Thanksgiving**

34

Father, it is right for us to give you thanks and praise.
Even though you are the God of all eternity, you
          have not left us to struggle on our own. You
          have acted so decisively for us in Jesus our
          saviour.
We thank you that when we are too hurt to forgive
          others, you are overflowing with mercy to all;
    when we are too callous to notice the pain of
          others, you feel it in yourself;
    when life bewilders us and we do not know what
          the good is, you maintain your righteous will;
    when we are at our weakest, in pain or doubt or
          distress or self-pity, you know our frailty but
          remain strong for us;
    when we want to run away from life, you keep
          with us and hold resolutely to your purposes
          of love.
Therefore with angels and archangels and with all the

company of heaven, we laud and magnify
your glorious name, evermore praising you
and saying:
HOLY, HOLY, HOLY,
LORD GOD OF HOSTS,
HEAVEN AND EARTH ARE FULL OF YOUR GLORY,
GLORY BE TO YOU, O LORD MOST HIGH.
AMEN.

(T G L)

35

O Jesus Christ, you are our Saviour because you have
chosen us.
We did not choose you: but in our weakness and
failure you loved us and wanted us and called
us and sent us.
Thanks be to God for the gospel of grace.
O Jesus Christ, you are our Master because you have
taught us and commanded us.
From you we have learned of God's forgiveness
and known that we too are to forgive. From
you we have learned of love and know that we
are to love one another. From you we have
learned of the power of God coming suddenly
and irresistibly and we have known in whom
we are to trust.
Thanks be to God for the gospel of his kingdom.
O Jesus Christ, you are our Friend because you have
given us another to be our Advocate, helper
and encourager. The Spirit of truth is with us
now to plead our cause, to get us through and
to find our best.
Thanks be to God for the gospel of his Spirit.

O Jesus Christ, our Saviour, Master and Friend, hear
our thanksgiving and hear us praying in your
words: *Our Father....*

(A R C M)

36

Mysterious and loving God, you move where you will,
creating, changing, making all things new, making us
new, like a dusty street washed clean by rain, like a
wind carrying the scent of water and grass, like the
wonder on the face of a child. We give thanks that
always, in you, we have the possibility of new life, new
hope, new clarity. You call us to love, you move us to
see you in every leaf and blade of grass, in every sound
and movement, in every encounter with others, in
every act of goodness, in the pain and pleasure of
every moment and every day. Your love will burn
like a fire within us, melting our frozen hearts, calling
us painfully and ecstatically into life, revealing Christ
among us, crucified, risen, and present in every place
and part of our daily existence. We give you thanks for
loving us enough so that we, broken people, may see
you in life transformed, so that the desert of emptiness
and despair may become the valley of delight.

Mysterious and loving God, you are found everywhere, and you call us to meet you in the need of
other, to see your face in the twisted faces of the
hungry
——in the angry faces of the oppressed
——in the fearful faces of the violent
——in the worn faces of the sick
——in the sad faces of the lonely

—in the dear faces of the beloved
—in the fresh faces of children
—in the unknown faces of the strangers.
And as we see you in them, may we welcome them,
As we meet you in them, may we respond to them,
As we know you in them, may we bless them,
In your name, for you.

(K G and I G)

37

God our Father, we thank you for your continued purpose for the world that all should live in harmony with you.

Jesus Christ, our Lord, we thank you for your compelling witness brought through word and action, which broke down the dividing walls of hostility between people and made possible the founding of the Church.

Holy Spirit, the Counsellor, we thank you for your continued presence in the Church and in the world, keeping alive the loving work of God through the body of Christ.

Eternal community of the Trinity, we thank you that your pattern of community is the pattern you wish for your Church and for the world.

Hear us as we pray as part of these communities of Church and world.

We pray for those who hang back from community because they are afraid that they will either be overwhelmed or rejected: those who are compelled to live a life of loneliness, cut off from the comfort and encouragement of real companionship; grant them the vision of your gentle, fulfilling friendship.

We pray for the Church, so often divided, and in its dividedness unable to reflect either the community

of the Trinity or the community which is your purpose
for the world. Grant to the Churches a vision of your
healing, reconciling Kingdom, and through your
Spirit, enable them to work towards the fulfilment of
that vision.

We pray for the world, so torn apart by strife.
Especially this week we pray for....We pray that the
divisions of the nations may be overcome in sensitive
government in compassionate, selfless concern for the
needs of the poorest and weakest of their people.

Grant to us and to the world, a vision of real
peace: let peace fill our hearts, our world, our
universe.

(S M K)

38

Gracious and eternal God,
Time past, other gods, and not you, have ruled over
        us.
But we have choked on the stones
    that they offered us as bread,
    we have sunk in the sand
    that they camouflaged as rock,
    we have known the futility
    that they described as fulfilment,
    we have experienced the illusion
    that they dressed up as reality,
    we have seen the glitter
    that they passed off as light,
    we have escaped from the death
    that they assured us was life.
So always we come back to you,
    like a prodigal returning,
    for you are our home.

Where would we be without you?
Where would we be
   without that knowledge of you
   made known to us in Jesus your son
   but on a pointless journey,
   travelling a road going nowhere,
   locked in on ourselves,
   consumed by haunting regret,
   in a valley of dry bones,
   denied breath of new life,
   imprisoned in emptiness,
   anticipating nothing at the end?
Praise be that where we are now
   is living in you,
   for you have come to dwell in us, among us,
   through Jesus Christ, our Lord.
   Tear the clouds apart
   and be seen again to live in your world.
   Break gently down the doors
   of those who are distanced from you
   and yet desperately most need you—
   those stunned and shocked by death,
   widows, widowers, and orphaned children;
   those who cannot ever see
   how they can put their lives together again;
   those who suffer ongoing remorse
   because of what they have done
   or failed to do;
   those whose conscience goes on accusing them
   so that they cannot find forgiveness.
   Touch the sick with your healing hands,
   sustain the terminally ill,
   and comfort the dying,
   through Jesus Christ our Lord,
   in whose words we pray together: *Our Father. . . .*

(R F B)

(iv)   **Prayers of Intercession**

39

Almighty God, gracious Father,
>   in the presence of your bounty, keep us humble,
>   in the presence of all men's needs make us
>   compassionate and caring.

Give us faith in our praying and love in our serving, knowing that by your power, all may find a new balance in living and a new victory in adversity.

We pray for all unhappy lives, those who are bitter and resentful, feeling life has given them a raw deal, those who are sensitive to criticism and quick to take offence, those who desire their own way, whatever the inconvenience or cost to other.

May your judgement and mercy be for their healing.

We pray for those who are lonely, who are shy and self-conscious, who find it hard to make friends, those who are nervous and timid, who ever feel themselves strangers in a world they can scarce understand.

May your presence inspire confidence and ensure companionship.

We pray for those who live with bitter regrets, for loving relationships brought to ruin, for opportunities freely given and woefully abused, for the bitterness of defeat or betrayal at another's hand or for failure in personal integrity.

May your grace give new hope to find victory in the very scene of failure.

We pray for all in illness and pain, weary of the day and fearful of the night. Grant healing if it be your will, and at all times through faith the gift of your indwelling place.

Bless the company of Christ's folk, the Church in

every land. Make her eager in worship, fearless in proclamation of the Gospel and passionate for caring.

Bless our country. Bless our leaders. Bless our children and grant us peace within our borders. Grant us as a nation to be found effective in establishing peace throughout the world.

Bless us each one in the communion of your saints and keep us ever mindful of the great cloud of witnesses that, following in their steps, as they did in the steps of the Master, we may with them at the last receive the fulfilment promised to your people.

Through Jesus Christ, our Lord.

(A B D)

40

Accept, O God, the gifts of our hands and the dedication of our hearts, and with our gifts receive now our prayers to all those to whom we are bound by our common humanity and our common need.

We pray, O God, in the name of Christ, who came to break down barriers and to reconcile mankind to one another and to their God. We pray for nations and for leaders of the nations. We pray for places we have not been to and people we do not know, part of that world for love of which Christ came, part of that humanity for love of whom his arms were stretched out. For the hungry and the oppressed, for prisoners of conscience, for the weak and the inarticulate. For those who yearn for peace and all who seek to make peace. For all who cannot see ground to believe in a God who cares or in a Christ who lives. For our own nation in its perplexities and its splintered loyalties, that we may discover unity of purpose and true prosperity, justice for our people.

We pray for the Church, O God, that she may in your name do that work which will show her to be the Church indeed. Give her power, not as the world knows power, but the power to love, the power to live and the power to die. The fellowship of his suffering, the conformity to his death, that thereby she may find the power of his resurrection.

We pray for our sick and anxious people. For those who know themselves at hazard over their jobs, over their finances, over their marriages, over their way of life, over their faith, that they may find renewal and redirection by your grace.

We pray for all those who are seeking reality in their lives and do not know where to find it: those who are seeking meaning for their lives and do not know where to find that either; those who have not come to terms with life as it is, with its pain and frustration, as well as its moments of delight and fulfilment, who expect too much, who ask that night should never encroach upon the day, nor any cloud ever appear in the sky; and those who expect too little, who have not yet come to terms with newness of life, the energy released by forgiveness, and the power of the spirit to make all things new.

We thankfully remember those whose lives most significantly moulded our lives till their day was ended. Their warfare is accomplished, their pilgrimage completed, and now they see us still and love us still. Keep us one with them, and with all the faithful, going with us one day to the place of seeing and knowing and worshipping through Jesus Christ our Lord, to whom with the Father and the Holy Spirit we ascribe might, majesty, dominion and power, now and forevermore.

(W J G M)

41

We pray for people with special difficulties in coping
with life, and perhaps we are praying for each
other . . .
for people who find small children too much
to handle;
for small children subjected to abuse and treated
without imagination or without love;
for parents harrassed by teenagers;
for teenagers harrassed by parents;
for people for whom marriage has turned out to
be different from what they hoped;
for people for whom financial achievement has
not created peace of mind;
for people whose hope for retirement has been
blighted by ill-health;
for those whose dreams of the future have been
blighted by the loss of the one the future was
to have been shared with;
for those who turn now in their distress to you; for
those who in their distress cannot bear to turn
even to you;
for some who are not here to offer their own
prayers, whose needs we are constrained
ourselves to set before you, whose names are
on our lips now . . . .

(W J G M)

42

The harvest of the Spirit is love, joy and peace.
We bring before you, God almighty and all-
merciful, those whose lives give us love, whose faces

give us joy, whose words give us peace. Beyond our own circle there are those who work for love and share joy and witness for peace in the world. We bring also those who are starved of love, who have forgotten joy, who have never known peace.

Lord in your mercy, hear our prayer.

The harvest of the Spirit is patience, kindness and goodness.

We bring before you, O God, those whose patience has been an example to us, whose kindness has made us better, whose goodness has warmed the world. We also bring before you those who find patience hard and who long to be more patient; and those who never know kindness in their loneliness or disability or prison or hunger; and those who do not believe that there is any real goodness in the world.

Lord in your mercy, hear our prayer.

The harvest of the Spirit is fidelity, gentleness and self-control.

We bring before you, O God, those who have kept the faith of the Church and who have made our believing easier; and those whose gentleness has made us more gentle, and those whose self-control has worked for reconciliation and harmony. We also bring before you those who no longer believe, who never did believe, or who do not know if they believe; and those who suffer when others are not gentle: battered wives, victims of violence and religious bigotry; and those who struggle for self-control, who have a difficult nature to master.

Lord in your mercy, hear our prayer.

(A R C M)

43

The Church's one foundation
Is Jesus Christ her Lord.
O God our rock and our fortress
We praise you that your Church is built
On a foundation that will not pass away.
On Jesus Christ the apostles and prophets have built:
We too have been built into your Church:
And now we too must share the building.

So give us and all your Church
The hardness of granite and the tenderness of violets.
Give the elders of the Church
The wisdom of serpents and the harmlessness of
            doves.
May this week's work done among young people by
            your Church in your name
Be done to your glory.

God save the Queen.
Lead your leaders in the paths of righteousness
That all our people may love justice, mercy and peace.
Heal the sick; feed the hungry;
Strengthen the dying; bring hope to the bereaved.

We call to mind before you, O God, all those whom
you have given to be near and dear to us, and all for
whom we are especially bound to pray, asking you to
remember them for all good. We commend to you any
who may have wronged us by word or deed, asking
you to forgive them and us all our sins and to bring
them and us to your heavenly kingdom.

 Through Jesus Christ our Lord, in whose name
and words we pray saying: *Our Father....*

(A R C M)

44

God of the still, small voice,
in the stillness we seek your calming presence.
We seek it for ourselves and for our world,
toss and turned, shaken and broken, tormented and
        destroyed.
We seek it after all the physical and emotional forces of
        life have done their worst—
in the stillness after the wind, the earthquake and the
        fire.
Create for us that stillness,
take from our souls the strain and stress,
so that we may be more ready for you.
SILENCE

We pray for those whose stillness is broken by loss of
        any kind:
the loss of a loved one,
the loss of a job,
the loss of health;
for young people overwhelmed with a sense of
        hopelessness
and for the elderly who have lost their youthful
        visions,
and for all who bear the burden of loneliness.
In the stillness, we remember them, and pray that they
        may know the calm of your presence with
        them.
SILENCE

We pray for those who live in constant anxiety
dreading what the future might hold for them,
afraid to raise their hopes for better things to come lest
        they should be further disappointed.
We pray for those who suffer poverty—
those too poor to enjoy even the occasional luxury,

those uncertain where their next meal will come from;
the homeless and the unloved.
In the stillness, we remember them, and pray that they
may know the calm of your presence with
them in their struggle.
SILENCE

We pray for those involved in crimes of violence,
for those in countries divided by war and unrest,
for those divided by prejudice, where one treats
another as less than human.
In the stillness, we confess our part in the world's sin
and pray for peace.
SILENCE

And we pray for the Church
that it may truly speak with the voice of Christ.
Make it vulnerable, that it may speak with calm
humility;
make it outward-looking, that it may care deeply;
make it a community of peace-makers and bridge-
builders,
that in the midst of life's turbulence
it may make space for the hearing of your still, small
voice.
SILENCE

Lord, hear our prayer.

(S M K)

45

Lord God, in this time of worship we set aside time for
silence,

a time to be still and know that you are God.
In silence let us know you in the beauty of creation,
    in the majesty of the mountains
    in the power of the sea,
    in the livelihood of the land
    in the creative skills of our hands
    in the enterprise of industry.
SILENCE
Lord in the silence, we give you thanks.

In silence, let us know you
    involved, suffering, aching,
    in the torment of disease,
    in the agony of the hospital bed,
    in the forsaken cry of the helpless,
    in the pleading eyes of the hungry,
    in the gaping sorrow of the bereaved,
    in the silent screams of the lonely.
SILENCE
Lord, in the stillness, we see your cross made real
      before us.

In silence, let us know you
    forgiving, caring, reconciling
    in the person who is there to listen,
    in the word of encouragement,
    in the skill of the nurse, the doctor, the social
      worker,
    in the sharing of knowledge and skills between
      nations,
    in the witness of the Church in the midst of
      today's needs.
SILENCE

Lord, in the quietness, we commit ourselves to
      involvement with you in the world you have
      made.

Enable us to see things from your perspective
that we may know a deeper meaning in life.
Let us be still and know that you are God,
creating, suffering, caring, and triumphant.
Let us return from this place
in the knowledge that your purpose will be
fulfilled
that love will triumph
that Resurrection means life and celebration and
freedom.
SILENCE

Through the refreshment and renewal of this time for
silence
enable us to reflect your presence and involvement
with us
and the whole world you have created.
In Jesus' name we pray.

(S M K)

46

A Prayer for our own community
Father in heaven, today we pray for this community in
which we live, that more and more we may feel our
belonging together, our need of each other, and the
strength and delight that comes from working and
striving together in common purpose....
Lord, help us to cultivate the gifts which abound
in our community.
Help us to be great encouragers.
Help us to be aware of each other's talents and
strengths.

Help us to be *for* each other, committed to each
    other's growth...
Help us to raise the level of confidence, and to
    awaken the spirit of service, so that generosity
    and laughter overflow....

(D T R)

47

O Lord our God, we believe your love to be broad
enough to embrace the remotest need, and deep
enough to reach the bitterest hurt; hear us as we align
ourselves with your compassion and pray for those we
know to be in need today:

For all who seek peace with justice in our world:
where war rages or oppression reigns or violence
threatens; where the poor are exploited, where
industrial relations are at breaking-point and where
human rights are denied:

LORD IN YOUR MERCY, HEAR OUR PRAYER

For all who through deprivation or unemployment can see little point or purpose in life, especially
the young and the disabled: and for all with the power
to help them if they would:

LORD IN YOUR MERCY, HEAR OUR PRAYER

For all who have dedicated their lives to serve you,
by the way they live and the work they do spreading the
good news of Jesus among all men, women and children on earth, for your Church in every denomination:

LORD IN YOUR MERCY, HEAR OUR PRAYER

For all schools and universities, that true learning,
with compassion and imagination, may be eagerly
sought and early found...

LORD IN YOUR MERCY, HEAR OUR PRAYER

For children everywhere, and for our families, friends and loved ones, wherever they may be:
LORD IN YOUR MERCY, HEAR OUR PRAYER
And hear our prayer for all in whom trust has been placed, all to whom power is given, all for whom love is asked, all through whom wisdom is sought and all by whom joy can come, because of Jesus our Lord:
To whom with you, our Father, and the Holy Spirit be praise and adoration from the whole Church, past, present and future, now and forever.

(D W D S)

48

Lord, you are to be found everywhere. Your Spirit is active in all the world. We see you in the dynamic forces of continuing creation. We hear you in the conversation of friends, the arguments that reveal truth, the debate among nations. You are present in the laboratory and lecture room, in research, and all human thoughtfulness. Whenever a hand is offered in friendship, a voice speaks in welcome, or eyes reflect forgiveness, you are there.

Spirit of God, you work within and beyond our experience: here in worship we ask for your gifts for our world:

for peace where there is no peace,
for joy where there are tears,
for health where there is sickness,
for youthfulness where there is age,
for food where there is famine,
for friendship where there is loneliness,
for beauty where there is ugliness,
for housing where there are refugees.

As you have shared your creative gifts with us, O God, so help us to share with others, using hand and eye, mind and skill, friendship and love, for the good of others and for the sake of Jesus Christ your Son and our Lord.

(T G L)

49

Father, we pray for this tried and troubled world, tormented as it is by human faithlessness and ill-will. We pray for justice and fair dealing between person and person; for an end to cheating and mistrust; to selfish taking-of-advantage and the refusal of self-sacrifice. We pray that the poor and helpless, those who cannot fight their own battles or shout for their own rights, may receive justice and be saved from loneliness and despair. And we pray that increasingly men and women, governments and nations, may stop seeking false security in force of arms or increasing wealth, and find instead all their promise for the future through faith in your goodness and commitment to your truth.

We know, Father, that these prayers of ours will not be answered at all, unless we begin to be their answer by the quality of our own lives. Help us, then, with all other Christians, to open our hearts to our fellow men and women, and our minds to the truth about them, so that we may be, for them, signs of your judgement and mercy.

So finally we pray for our families and friends, wherever they may be. Keep us faithful to them as you are always keeping faith with your world, where you reign, with your Son and the Holy Spirit, ever one God, world without end.

(T G L)

50

Lord Jesus Christ, if we speak in your name blind men's eyes will be opened, the deaf will hear, the lame will leap, the dumb will laugh and shout, and your people will come to you crowned with gladness, escorted by joy—sorrow and weariness will fly away.

Help us hold on to our dreams. Make us wild and free with the hope you have planted in us; ready to face the music, or take the consequences of being what we are, Christ's fools, believing the unbelievable, reaching out for the unattainable, trusting the things beyond seeing, the things beyond hearing, and the things beyond imagining that you have prepared for those who love you.

So, Lord, make us peace-makers, healers, comforters, giving hope to the hopeless, joy to the sad, courage to the weak, humility to the strong, repentance to the cruel and love to the hateful; until the people who walk in darkness see the great light and are glad and free, and there is no hurt or destruction in all your universe, because all know you and love you and honour you.

Father, we pray for all guilty men and women: those weighed down and those unaware; those who make freshness stale; those who make beauty foul; those who use strength to crush their neighbours; those who make affluence an affront to your holiness by their exploitation or neglect of other people's poverty or pain.

Lord God, make your world fresh and new and full of promise again. Let there be healing, light and peace. Let your Son's Church praise you and honour you as it serves humanity and proclaims your forgiveness. Let your world, your universe, your immeasurable creation join in the chorus of praise: through Jesus Christ our Lord.

(T G L)

(v) **Closing Prayers**

51

Lord of creation
    we are grateful for this day
    and all the music of it—
    a gift of joy springing
    into the life of the world.
Help us to be transmitters of life,
    released from greed and self-concern,
    overflowing with generosity,
    bubbling with laughter and fun,
    rippling with music.
Link your life to ours, O Lord.
May the great river of your Spirit
    flow through us and across the world
    to fill the universe and every human heart
    till joy be unconfined,
    through Jesus Christ our Lord.
'The Grace ... and for evermore. Amen.'

(D T R)

52

Lord, the world is made by your hand, and kept
      moving by your power.
  Beyond our sight and beyond our understanding,
  there you are.
  Where the light of distant stars begins, in the
      darkness of space,
  there you are.
  In our hearts and beside us,
  there you are.
  In our loneliness and when we think ourselves to
      be unobserved and forgotten,
  there you are.
Lord God, once in Jesus Christ you came:
  and mankind saw you and heard you and knew
      you.
  Still in him, you come, and we hear your voice.
  Help us to walk through this world in your
      strength;
  to live in your service; to claim your help; and to
      do your will;
  that in this world, as in a myriad of other worlds,
  your will may be done.

(W J G M)

53

(a) *Dedication of Offerings*

Gracious God and Father, giver of every good and
perfect gift, be pleased to accept these offerings of our
hearts that we bring to you. Bless them and multiply

them in usefulness for the service of your Kirk and Kingdom; and with them receive the love of our hearts and the service of our lives this day and always.

(b) *Dedication of Offerings*

Gracious Father, we acknowledge the gifts that daily flow from you to satisfy our needs and enrich our lives.
    As we accept them humbly, enlarge our hearts with love, that our giving at this time may be a token of thanksgiving and a pledge of concern. Hasten our going forth on the errands of your mercy for the needs of all mankind and the extension of your Kingdom.

(A B D)

54

Father, may your world be yours indeed,
your will be ours,
your benediction come on all our living and loving,
thinking and doing,
to the glory of your name
and our eternal peace.

(T G L)

55

Like your disciples on the road to Emmaus, we are so often incapable of seeing that you, O Christ, are our companion on the way.

But when our eyes are opened we realise that you were speaking to us even though perhaps we had forgotten you. Then, the sign of our trust in you is that, in our turn, we try to love and forgive with you. Independently of our doubts or even of our faith, you, O Christ, are always present: your love burns in our heart of hearts. Send us out in the power of your Spirit to live and work to your praise and glory.

(T G L)

56

Closing Responses

Leader: On our heads and our houses
All: THE BLESSING OF GOD
Leader: In our coming and going
All: THE PEACE OF GOD
Leader: In our life and believing
All: THE LOVE OF GOD
Leader: At our end and new beginning
All: THE ARMS OF GOD TO WELCOME US AND
BRING US HOME.
AMEN.

(K G and I G)

(vi) Complete Prayers for Sunday Services

57

Call to Prayer and First Prayer

Leader: Come, let us return to the Lord,
for he has torn us and will heal us,
he has struck us
and he will bind up our wounds.

All: AFTER TWO DAYS HE WILL REVIVE US,
ON THE THIRD DAY HE WILL RESTORE US,
THAT IN HIS PRESENCE WE MAY LIVE.

Leader: Let us humble ourselves,
let us strive to know the Lord,
whose justice dawns like morning light,
its dawning as sure as the sunrise.

All: HE WILL COME TO US LIKE A SHOWER,
LIKE SPRING RAINS THAT WATER THE
EARTH.

Leader: Gracious and eternal God.
It is an invitation we can hardly believe—
in a world where people are striving to
impress and straining to achieve,
where value is accorded to those with the
symbols and trappings
of riches and honour and power and
distinction,
you say to us simply:
Come, just as you are,
with all your faults and failings,
and I will give you fullness of life.

All: LET US HUMBLE OURSELVES
AND TURN TO GOD,
WITH BROKEN AND CONTRITE HEARTS,
THAT HE MIGHT GIVE US THE LIFE OF JESUS
HIS SON.

Leader: It is a world we can scarcely trust—
in a world where everything has a price and
anything can be bought,
where people can be persuaded
to do all kinds of things
for money or success or status or prestige,
you whisper to us softly:
Come, just as you are,
without money and without price,
and I will give you abundant life.

All: LET US HUMBLE OURSELVES
AND TURN TO GOD,
WITH OPEN AND EMPTY HANDS,
THAT HE MIGHT GIVE US THE LIFE OF JESUS
HIS SON.

Leader: It is a promise we can barely credit—
in a world where might is right
and force is strength;
where people are driven by egotism
and suspicion and fear
to dominate and manipulate and use and
control,
you speak to us gently:
Come, just as you are,
with all your weakness and vulnerability,
and I will make you fishers of men.

All: LET US HUMBLE OURSELVES
AND TURN TO GOD,
DRAW NEAR TO HIM AS HE WOULD DRAW
NEAR TO US,
THAT HE MIGHT GIVE US THE LIFE OF JESUS
HIS SON.
AMEN.

Prayers of Gratitude and Concern

Leader: Gracious and ever living God,
Your promise to us is that,
when we are old and our hairs are grey,
you will not forsake us,
but will be ever with us and for us.
Be with those today
who are old and alone, neglected and forgotten,
and who anticipate tomorrow with the foreboding that
they will be as lonely then
as they were yesterday and today.
Be with those today
whose special calling is the care of the elderly, in home or in hospital.
that they might share understanding and dignity.

All: IN ALL HIS PROMISES, GOD KEEPS FAITH
AND EVERYTHING HE DOES IS GOOD.

Leader: Your promise to us is this:
when we feel frail and inadequate,
you will send us your spirit to enable us
to stand for your truth and speak in your name.
Be with those today,
whose courage is failing and whose confidence is gone,
and who sense that the same temptations
and the same sins
that brought them down in the past
will bring them down again in the future.
Be with those today
whose special skill is to be
carriers of healing and bearers of forgiveness, that they might create a climate of compassion and hope.

All: IN ALL HIS PROMISES, GOD KEEPS FAITH,
AND EVERYTHING HE DOES IS GOOD.

Leader: Your promise to us is that
when we are exploited and oppressed
you will know our suffering and heed our
affliction,
and will come and set us free.
Be with those today
who are removed and imprisoned, tortured
and abused,
and who know that the road to freedom may
be very long, and may not be travelled till
long after they are gone.
Be with those today
whose special ministry is
to bear witness to the light in the deepest
darkness,
that they might be signs of your coming
Kingdom.

All: IN ALL HIS PROMISES, GOD KEEPS FAITH,
AND EVERYTHING HE DOES IS GOOD.
MAY WE TRUST HIS PROMISES
AND LIVE BY HIS GRACE,
SO THAT WE ALSO MAY DO GOOD,
IN THE NAME AND FOR THE SAKE
OF JESUS CHRIST, OUR LORD,
IN WHOSE WORDS WE FURTHER PRAY
SAYING, *OUR FATHER....*

Prayers for Dedication of the Offering
All: LORD, WE CANNOT GIVE MORE
THAN WE HAVE RECEIVED,
BUT YOU HAVE GIVEN US EVERYTHING,
IN JESUS, YOUR SON.
OUR OFFERING IS A SIGN THAT, IN RETURN,

WE GIVE ALL THAT WE ARE AND ALL THAT
WE HAVE
TO SERVE YOUR PURPOSE FOR THE WORLD
MADE KNOWN IN JESUS.
AMEN.

(R F B)

58

Eternal God, the vast created universe declares your
glory; the hosts of heaven worship your majesty; the
whole earth exalts your holy Name.

Father, we come here to find peace at the point
where the rushing stream of life pauses, and to learn
more about your love for us in Jesus Christ our Lord.

Let us confess our sins to God.

Loving God, we read of your mighty acts among
your people, and we rejoice in your power displayed in
Jesus.

We confess our faithlessness and lack of trust. We
have lived as though your power belonged to the past;
we have not trusted Jesus to work miracles of healing
and forgiveness in us; we've looked at our own sin,
we've been frightened by it; when we've looked at the
sin of others, it has made us smug. In the silence of
our hearts and in the company of those around us we
remember now how and where and when we have
sinned in thought and word and deed.

Lord, have mercy upon us:

CHRIST, HAVE MERCY UPON US: LORD, HAVE
MERCY UPON US.

May the Almighty and merciful Father grant to
each one of you pardon, absolution and remission of
all your sins, time for amendment of life and the grace

and comfort of his Holy Spirit; through Jesus Christ our Lord.

Father, we pray for miracles: not miracles that make people throw up their hands in bewildered admiration; not miracles of love; true signs of your Spirit at work in the world, changing hearts and minds, leading us on and on in the ways of peace. We pray for miracles in the life of the Church: miracles that break through hard-heartedness and hard-headedness, opening our hearts and minds to other peoples' truth. We pray for miracles in the life of the world: the miracle of justice, peace and healing and wholeness for every person. We pray for humble greatness in the world's politicians; for the will and ability in them to achieve just ends by peaceful means.

And we pray for joy and gladness in the lives of those who are overwhelmed with misery now; abundance for those who live in poverty now; blooming good health and maturing strength, for those who are ill or in despair.

We pray that people who are considered useless or hopeless now, may be given their full value as human beings; that those who are severely handicapped, mentally, physically or emotionally, may be enabled to achieve their full potential, find joy and give joy to others.

Feed us now, Lord Jesus Christ, as you fed your disciples long ago: let us never be hungry or thirst again, as your love springs up in us, for eternal life, where you live and reign with the Father, in the unity of the Spirit, one God for ever and ever.

Prayers of Thanksgiving
> The Lord be with you:
> AND WITH THY SPIRIT.

Lift up your hearts:
WE LIFT THEM UP UNTO THE LORD.
Let us give thanks unto the Lord our God:
IT IS MEET AND RIGHT SO TO DO.

Father, it is right for us to give you thanks and praise, for your glory displayed in the world and for all your wonderful works. We thank you for the daily miracles of sight and hearing by which we know and rejoice in your creating power. We thank you for the continual renewal of the earth, for your constant activity in the processes of life.

We thank you for your glory displayed in Jesus. We thank you, too, for the miracle of love offered to the undeserving, of you at work in human life. We thank you for his humble birth, for the power of love revealed in his living and his dying, in his resurrection and ascension, in the coming of his holy and life-giving Spirit.

Especially, we thank you...and that in Jesus you have fed us with the bread of life. Therefore, with angels and archangels and with all the company of heaven, we laud and magnify your glorious name, evermore praising you and saying:

HOLY, HOLY, HOLY,
LORD GOD OF HOSTS,
HEAVEN AND EARTH ARE FULL OF THY GLORY,
GLORY BE TO THEE, O LORD MOST HIGH.
AMEN.
Our Father....

Lord Jesus, you said: Ask and you will receive, the door will be opened; give our hearts such love this night, that our whole lives be inspired by it, in all that we do, and that we never tire of praising you with the Father and the Holy Spirit now and for ever.

(T G L)

59

Prayers for use in Morning and Evening Worship

Almighty God our Father,
>   out of love that cannot be measured you have
>   created the heavens and the earth;
>   out of grace that cannot be exhausted you sustain
>   your created order;
>   out of wisdom that cannot be plumbed you direct
>   the affairs of people;
>   into light that cannot be extinguished you receive
>   your own.
We worship you, the one who is the source of all love,
grace, wisdom and light and we praise you that our worship is acceptable and pleasing to you, through the Lord
Jesus Christ. In him, we see your love practised, your
grace evidenced, your wisdom revealed, your light shine.
    Too often we are without love, ungracious, foolish
and wandering in darkness. We live in our own
confusion and it is a cold fearsome place. Lift our eyes
to your son, the Christ of Calvary, in all his stark
loneliness that we might know
>   the sweetness of being forgiven,
>   the fragrance of being accepted,
>   the power of being set free for service,
>   the joy of being strengthened in faith.
In the warm fellowship of your people awakened by
>   the Holy Spirit
>   refresh us and renew us,
>   challenge us and change us
that, resting in the warm cradle of our Father's love,
we may be channels of the love, grace, wisdom and
light of the Lord Jesus, that his kingdom may be
displayed and his Church re-created
>   through him who served in humility
>   and reigns in glory
ever Jesus Christ our Lord.   Amen.

The magnificent order and unfathomable splendour of the universe speak clearly of your majestic power, O God. The delicate beauty of a flower and the sheer tenderness of the new-born baby proclaim your intimate love for all that is the creation of your hands.

Lord of power and love, from a world that toils in the helplessness of human weakness and the apathy of human indifference, the cry goes out for help and we take that cry upon our lips through Jesus Christ our Lord.

Lord of all wisdom, whose purpose for the world is beautiful and glorious, there is in your world so much confusion, ugliness and darkness that threatens to thwart the fulfilment of your purpose.

Come in the simplicity of your wisdom into the complexity of this world that our Queen, our government and all who guide the nations would know the clarity and beauty and light of your mind, and so lead us all to that place of unity and peace through Jesus Christ our Lord.

Lord of all power evidenced in the dependence of a cradle and the weakness of a cross, there is in your world so much corrupted power, seen in the careless suppression of the powerless and the selfish manipulation of the weak. Too often, human dignity is the captive of human greed.

Come in the power of your love that lives and that cannot die to free us from the snare of our greed and set our feet on the straight road that leads to justice and equity and to the restoration of human dignity for all people through Jesus Christ our Lord.

Lord of all comfort from whom we come and to whom we must return, there is in your world still the divisive shadow of death hanging over broken hearted families. You have promised us the Comforter and your comfort is rooted in your victory over death.

Come and shine in the strength of your comfort

into the dark corners of broken hearts and fill them with the brightness of your victory and the assurance of eternal life through Jesus Christ our Lord.

Lord of all compassion you journeyed from Bethlehem through Nazareth to Jerusalem and so you feel with us and for us.

There is in your world, sickness and uncleanness and hunger. You heal the sick, you touch the unclean, you feed the hungry.

Come in the gentleness of your authority so that lives diseased would know the peace of your presence through Jesus Christ our Lord.

So make your Church, O Lord of wisdom, power, comfort and compassion, the instrument of your all embracing love, the testimony of your reconciling love, the channel of your healing love, the proclaimer of your saving love, that through her devotion to Christ and his world, the Kingdoms of this world would become truly the Kingdoms of our God.

Through Jesus Christ our Lord to whom with you, our Father and the Holy Spirit be all glory and praise, world without end. Amen.

(N M)

60

Especially in rural places, in parishes where there are a number of separate churches, it might frequently be necessary to authorise local elders to conduct worship in place of the minister. The following order might be used as a framework.

Let us worship God:

A Hymn or Psalm (of praise to God in his majesty and goodness).

They that wait on the Lord shall renew their strength. They shall mount up on wings as eagles. They shall run and not be weary. They shall walk and not faint.

Let us pray:
Almighty God, great, good and holy beyond our highest thoughts, who holds the whole world in your hand, we come into your Presence with reverence. May your Holy Spirit inspire us to reach out to you in our prayers, and to give to you, poor as we are, the love and worship of our whole heart and mind.

Our Heavenly Father, as we think of you, pure and holy, unlimited in love and goodness, we are aware of our selfishness, in which we seek our own comfort before our neighbour's need; our vanity, in which we imagine ourselves better than we are; we confess how weakly we yield to what we know is evil. We have sinned against you and against our brothers and sisters. Lord have mercy upon us.

We give thanks for the Gospel, that if we confess our sins there is forgiveness and blessing, through your great love and patience.

Forgive us, Holy Father, for all our sins. By your Holy Spirit renew our spirit. Make us honest in all our dealings. Teach us to forgive as we are forgiven and to love as we are loved; in the Name of our Lord Jesus Christ who died for us, and who taught us to pray saying: *Our Father....*

A Reading from the Old Testament
A Hymn (of devotion to Christ)
A Reading from the New Testament

Let us pray:
We give you thanks, our Heavenly Father, for the world that you have made: for its wonder and beauty and wealth; we give thanks for the powers you have given us to enjoy its loveliness and to be nourished

from its fruits; we praise you for Sabbath quiet and the company of those we love; for the wisdom of the wise, the courage of the brave and the goodness of your saints. We praise you for your living Word that stirs us from sleeping. In all our thankfulness we praise you, with your people in every land and in every language, for our Lord Jesus Christ, who is above all others to be loved and honoured.

Glory be to the Father and to the Son and to the Holy Spirit, as it was in the beginning, is now and ever shall be, world without end.

A prayer for the world.
Lord, when we are angry and dismayed at the cruelties of man to man, the blindness of governments, the follies of peoples; when we are humbled by our own disobedience to the truth we know; then we remember that you are the Father of all; we remember that Christ carries the sorrows of all; we believe that your Spirit strives in all men and women for truth and justice. Restore in us the confidence that your Kingdom is sure. Rebuke the violence of wicked and cruel men. Give peace in our time, O Lord.

A prayer for our own country and people.
God bless our land, our queen and her household. Give wisdom to the queen's ministers and guide them in the choices that lie before us today. May we not rest till there is a place of dignity and freedom in our land for young and old, weak and strong. May we find our unity in a revival of true reverence for you our God.

A prayer for our parish.
Heavenly Father, may we who are baptized into the Name of Jesus be his ministers in this place. Teach us in humility to offer our service to our neighbours and to have care for those in need. Bless the old among us.

Guard our youth and enable us to lead them in the Christian way. Give peace in our homes and may all who are anxious find an answer to their prayers, through Jesus Christ our Lord.

(Here may follow prayer for any special happenings or concerns in the minds of the people of the Parish.)

A Remembrance of those who have died in faith.
Eternal Father, we give thanks for all those who have worshipped here in times past, and have shown the love of Christ in their generation. Especially we give thanks for those dear to ourselves. Give us the same loyalty and courage in our days, and keep us at one with them in spirit, till our union with them is perfect and eternal. Through Jesus Christ our Lord, to whom with you the Father and with the Holy Spirit, One God, be glory and dominion world without end. AMEN.

At this point Intimations may be made.
A Hymn (invoking the guidance of the Holy Spirit).
Address or Sermon.

The Offering.
Almighty God, whose gifts to us are numberless, and whose supreme gift to us in our Lord Jesus Christ makes us for ever humble and thankful; we lay our offerings to you on your table with the prayer that they may be accepted as tokens of our love and worship, our loyalty and service, so long as we live; in the Name of Christ to whom be praise and dominion world without end. AMEN

A Hymn (of dedication and worship).
The Grace of our Lord Jesus Christ and the love of God and the communion of the Holy Spirit be with us all evermore. AMEN.

(J M)

61

Prayers for an ordinary Sunday Service.

'May the glory of the Lord last for ever! May the Lord be happy with what he has made.' (Psalm 104:31, TEV)

Eternal and glorious God, creator of the universe and maker of mankind, we come before you this day, hesitant and humble. For you are so far above us, sometime so much beyond us, that you seem unreal to us as a God who cares.

And yet in Jesus, you have become for us a loving Father, whose concern goes beyond mere words, to love in action.

In your son, you have shown us beyond misunderstanding that people matter, and that you want us to belong to your family. And still we are so conscious of our inadequacies, that we hesitate to seek to belong to your people. We stand aloof, fearful of further hurt. We stand apart, frightened that nobody loves us.

Our Father God, whose love is for us all, no matter what we have done; make real to us now your acceptance to us as people, helping us to recognise that while you condemn our sin, you always love the sinner.

Help us to accept ourselves now, as someone whom God loves...and chasten us when we reject ourselves, or condemn each other, for who are we to judge whom God loves.

O God in whose hands all justice and all judgements lie, help us not to be satisfied with ourselves. For you have set before us a standard in Jesus, which is patience, kindness and love.

Grant us an awareness of our faults, a burning desire to change them, and an ability through your strength to do something about them and be changed. As we accept your forgiveness, help us to forgive each other as we begin this day anew as part of your creation.

May we seek your glory, in the doing of our best in our daily lives, in caring for others, with patience and kindness, and in worshipping you, in faithfulness and in joy.

These things we ask in the name and for the sake of Jesus Christ our Lord, who taught us when we pray to say: *Our Father...*

Almighty and everlasting God, by whose hands everything exists, great is our thanksgiving for the diversity of your wonders. We know that we see only a little of your creation, and this for us is but a foretaste of the glorious beauty which is the whole. All of heaven and earth are your concern, and we rejoice that your care extends even to us, people who are far from perfect, and yet made in your image.

O Lord our God, we appreciate this world in which you have placed us. The daily miracles of nature, fresh every morning with the rising of the sun. The spider's web, etched in dew drops... like diamonds set on fire in the sparkling light. The trees bare branded in winter, starkly setting shape against an evening sky. In spring time promise breaking into bud. In summer dress, adorned with dancing leaves. In autumn, fruitfully dying in a blaze of glorious colour.

Against the setting of these beauties Lord, you have put mankind... in riches and in poverty, in sickness and in health, in justice and in oppression... friends with each other... at war with each other.

We give you thanks this day O Lord, for those who have as their daily habit something of your loving care for others ... people who work in slums and in soup kitchens, who nurse in hospitals and where there are no facilities ... Who stand up and are counted for what is right and is good, in the face of oppressive authority.

For their example we are grateful, as also we need their actions.

Our Father God, whose Son Jesus did come to set us free, we come to you now to pray for those in our day who stand for that which seeks the good of all people. May your strength and courage be with those who follow you truly, and seek to do your will; that their example be an inspiration for everyone who comes into contact with them.

Lord Jesus, you were such an attractive personality, that men and women sought you out, gladly and willingly sharing your company. We pray for those who draw others to you, through your light shining in them. May they always point beyond themselves to him who is the glory.

O glorious God, who has brought us order out of chaos, in this disintegrating society, we remember before you now, those who seek to put people back together again, all the counsellors, psychiatrists and therapists who work with individuals and with families. We pray for men and women whose lives are so shattered, and whose personalities are so splintered from the rest of society that they know not where or to whom they belong. We pray that they may come to know something of the order you can create in us all ... if first we believe in Jesus who is our friend.

O Lord, we pray for those in our own lives who have brought us security ... that safety of body and spirit whereby we are at home in ourselves and in you. Grant unto all who care, the perseverance and the persistence to pursue what is necessary to convince people that they matter ... and matter most of all to you.

And Father, we come to you, thankfully yours, and walking in the footsteps of your Son. Grant we pray, to all who seek you, the joy of faith, the determination of faithfulness, the comfort of peace, the certainty of love, and the hope of salvation, always giving thanks for those who have gone before us, and are now in your nearer presence.

In Jesus Christ our Lord. Amen.

(W F D)

Section II

Worship for the Seasons
of the Christian Year

(i) *Prayers for Advent*   *Page*
  1 Lewis   A Short Act of Worship for
                       the beginning of Advent   89
  2 McLellan   Prayers on Advent Themes:
                       (a) *Death*   91
                       (b) *Judgement*   94
                       (c) *Heaven*   95
                       (d) *Hell*   97
  3 Longmuir   Prayers for Bible Sunday (Second
                       in Advent)   100

(ii) *Prayers for Christmas*
  4 Ogston   Prayers for Christmas Eve   102
  5 McLellan   Confession for the Sunday
                       after Christmas   103
  6 Longmuir   Prayers for Epiphany   104
  7 Longmuir   Service for Candlemas   107

(iii) *Prayers for Lent and Easter*
  8 McLellan   Prayers for Seventh Sunday
                       before Easter   110
  9 Longmuir   Prayers for First Sunday in Lent   111
 10 Brown   Palm Sunday: 'Outreach'   114
 11 Matheson   A Service of Meditation for
                       Good Friday   117
 12 Campbell   Easter   120
 13 Longmuir   An Easter Prayer of Approach
                       and Confession   121
 14 W G M McDonald   Easter Prayer   122
 15 Ogston   An Easter Prayer of Approach   124

(iv) *Prayers for Pentecost*
 16 Brown   'Those who live...'   125
 17 Longmuir   'Let all the world praise you...   128

Worship for the Seasons
of the Christian Year

(i) Prayers for Advent

1

A Short Act of Worship for the beginning of Advent

HOSANNA IN THE HIGHEST! BLESSED IS HE WHO
COMES IN THE NAME OF THE LORD!

Reading: Isaiah 11, 12

Prayer: Lord Jesus, long-awaited Holy One of Israel,
and Saviour of the Gentiles also, if we were honest with
ourselves and you we would confess at once that we do
not really welcome your Advent, this year or any year.
We would prefer you not to come among us, to upset
our slumbers and disturb our equilibrium. Deep inside
each of us are stagnant, lukewarm pools of inertia,
complacency and disenchantment.

We acknowledge before you with shame that we
do not really hunger for the bread of your new life, or
thirst for the water of your messianic Spirit; we
entertain few dreams for the coming of your Kingdom,
and have little appetite for the cost and danger to
ourselves of its arrival.

Not only privately do we prefer the way things
are, hope to postpone your advent and intend to keep
you a little longer at arm's length. For the whole
Church, of which we are a part, has mostly ceased to

look and watch and wait; her capacity for expectation, her sense of eager longing, atrophied long since. She has made peace with the status quo, she has done deals with other powers and kingdoms; she has sought glory elsewhere than in your cross. We are all resigned to the safe assumption that your Father's will cannot be done on earth as it is in heaven.

Forgive all this acquiescence and contentment.

And as we gather up before you the needs of this community and of the wider Church, of this nation and of the wider world, we do not merely ask you to come and change either Church or world, but that first you would change us. Give us the courage to endure the pain of being changed, and the vigour and the vision to be agents of change ourselves. We do not pray only that you will come with messianic power to comfort the lonely, feed the hungry and heal the sick; we pray that first you will force us to see the brokenness and poverty of our own condition; that newly filled and healed ourselves, we might with heightened sensitivity be to others more effective channels of your wholeness and fulfilment.

We do not merely pray that you will come again as the New Moses, to liberate the enslaved and dispossessed still languishing in Egypt-like oppression; we pray that first you will set us free from our indifference, short-sightedness and self-preoccupation. Give us fresh boldness ourselves to face the Pharaohs of our world with the gospel demand that they should let your people go, and fresh energy ourselves to struggle in your name for their release.

Hear then our Advent prayers of hope and hesitation. We ask not only for signs that your kingdom is coming, but also for the strength and flexibility, the imagination and endurance, to cope with the consequences when our prayer is answered. Lord, we believe, but help our unbelief; we await, but help

our apprehension. And we pray together as you taught
us: *Our Father....*

Finally, we sing The Advent Hymn par excellence
—one version at least of the Magnificat of Mary—'Tell
out my soul the greatness of the Lord'.

(A L)

2

Prayers on Advent Themes

(a) *Death*

What will it be like to die?
It says in the Bible:
'Though I walk through the valley of the shadow of
          death I will fear no evil: for thou art with me.'

O God our help in ages past
Our hope for years to come
We frail creatures of a passing day
Know that you are from the first
And you are to the last.
Each day we die
And each day you are the living God
Living, and bringing us to life.

Bring us to life out of the death of our age
Out of despair and self-destructiveness and deep
          sadness
Bring us to joy
Bring us to life out of the death of the Church
Out of dull routine and frightened religion
Bring us to lively faith

Bring us to life out of the death of sin
Out of serving ourselves first, last, and all the time
Bring us to the freedom of serving you.

Bring us, O Lord God, at our last awakening
Into the house and gate of heaven,
To enter into that gate and dwell in that house,
Where there shall be no darkness nor dazzling,
But one equal light;
No noise nor silence, but one equal possession;
No ends nor beginnings, but one equal eternity;
In the habitations of your glory
And dominion world without end   (*John Donne*)
Amen.

Is there no justice?
It says in the Bible: 'The Lord comes to judge the
        earth: he shall judge the world with righteous-
        ness and the people with his truth'.

Come now, O Lord, to judge the world.
Come now, O Lord, to judge the world.
That evil may be punished, and wrong righted again
And the victims of injustice set free
For your judgement, O Lord, is just
Before you no lie can live for ever
No cruelty last for ever, no violence triumph for ever.
Come, O Lord, in judgement.

Yet never come.
For if you kept a record of our sins
Who could escape being condemned?
Everything you ask of us we have not done
And what you forbid has become our way of life.
We are guilty people:
Upon whom you declare the verdict:
'Innocent, made new, pardoned, forgiven, restored!'

Dealt with not as we have deserved,
But as you have loved and done.
Your ways are wonderful,
And your judgement beyond our understanding.

O Lord, because we often sin
And have to ask for pardon
Help us to forgive as we would be forgiven:
Neither mentioning old offences committed against us
Nor dwelling upon them in thought:
But loving others freely as you freely love us
For Jesus' sake
Amen.

For each of us, O God, there is the fear of dying
But in that fear is your promise: 'I will be with you',
Stronger than the fear.
For many of us, O God, there is the pain of separation
But in that pain is your promise: 'Where I am, you
          shall be',
Stronger than the pain.
For all of us, O God, there is the horror of war and
          famine
But in that horror is your promise: 'There shall be no
          more death, nor sorrow, nor crying'.

And we are led from horror to hope,
From death to life.
Let us give thanks to the God and Father of our Lord
          Jesus Christ
Who by his great mercy has given us new hope
By raising Jesus Christ from death.

God of all time, you are God not of the dead but of the
          living
For the dead are alive to you.
Abaham, Isaac and Jacob are your friends

Thomas More and John Knox and Martin Luther
        King
Are still your friends.
Our most precious memories, our dearest names
Are more than names and memories to you.
Death has not the strength to keep your children from
        you
For Jesus Christ, once dead, is dead no more
And death shall have no more dominion.
For the kingdom, the power and the glory
Are yours, and ours, forever.
Amen.

(b) *Judgement*

You came to judge the world
To bring light and cast out darkness
Once they brought you a temple coin and asked for
        judgement
So we bring to you our world of money
Share dealings, takeovers and taxes.
Our world of poverty and debt
Bring light and cast out darkness.

They told a story of seven brothers and one wife and
        asked you for judgement
So we bring to you our world of personal relationships
Marriage and divorce and family life
Our world of child abuse and bereavement
Bring light and cast out darkness.

They talked about neighbours and asked you for
        judgement
So we bring to you our world of neighbours
At work and home; our friends and family

Those we love; and, as you have taught us, our
        enemies.
Bring light and cast out darkness.

And once, Lord Jesus, you told a judgement story
Of sheep and goats: a story of compassion
So we bring you the hungry, the sick, and those
        in prison
And we bring our own compassion
Bring light and cast out darkness.

Then at the last
In the judgement hall of Pilate
Lord Jesus you stood silent and alone
As the world judged you.
Now, in the silence
Bring light and cast out darkness.

Even so, come Lord Jesus,
Amen.

(c) **Heaven**

What is there to hope for?
The Bible says about God's people:
'They desire a better country, that is, a heavenly one.
        Therefore God is not ashamed to be called
        their God, for he has prepared for them a
        city'.

Our Father, you are in heaven.
You are in heaven and we are on earth.
Yet your heaven will not stay away; but comes to us in
        hints and signs and hopes.
Your heaven breaks through the curtains of our dull
        lives, our earth bound lives

And makes us dream again, and yearn and hope.
We too desire a better country, a heavenly one
And we are glad to call you our God;
For you have prepared for us a city.

Oh how shallow is our hoping!
How selfish our dreams! How we long for the things
     that do not matter.
You offer us heaven; and we strive after earth without
     the nasty bits.
Set our feet on lofty places
So that we may hope and work and pray
For heaven which is your kingdom
The kingdom for which Jesus died and rose again.

When the dreamer of the Book of Revelation saw
     through a door
He glimpsed the heavenly city.
He saw the worship of heaven, the end of suffering
     and tears, and all things made new.
Grant us, O God, to look through that same door
And with wonder and hope approach it
That we may worship more truly,
Love more perfectly,
And live more gloriously.
Through Jesus Christ our Lord,
Amen.

Holy holy holy
Lord God of hosts
Heaven and earth are full of your glory.
We praise you for heaven's glories
For sins forgiven and death destroyed
For the promise that all tears shall be wiped away.
We praise you for the great company of the faithful
Those whom we have loved and those whom we have
     never known

Whose home is in heaven
Where all we have willed, or dreamed, or hoped of
   good shall exist.
We praise you for earth's glories
For beautiful things and lovely people
For patient love and lively memory and friends along
   the way.
Lord God of hosts, heaven and earth are full of your
   glory,
Since Jesus Christ is risen.

High king of heaven, the earth and all that it contains
   are yours
Yours are the disappointed dreamers, whose futures
   have turned to failure
Yours are the sour embittered ones, who hope no
   more.
So be their new birth, their new light.
Yours are the sick, the tortured, the suicidal
So hold them, and keep them, and love them as your
   own.
Yours, Lord God of hosts, are our own, the dear ones
   and the difficult
So bring them with us at the last.
To heaven where your will is done and your kingdom
   is come
For the sake of Jesus Christ our living hope,
Amen

(d) **Hell**

Where is there where God is not?
It says in the Bible:
'If I ascend up into heaven, thou art there: If I make
   my bed in hell, behold, thou art there'.

O Lord our God, in the darkest dark your light shines
    on
And the darkness has never been able to master it.
However far down, down, down
Underneath are the everlasting arms.
However alone, alone
Behold, you come to seek and to save
That which was lost.

But we are ashamed to be found
Guilty in the light, and preferring the cover of dark.
For you have made us for heaven, and we have
    yearned for hell.
Perversely, absurdly, we have lurched towards hell
We spend our money on the destruction of the world.
Our homes become battle grounds
We make cruelty an entertainment, and violence an art
    form.
O Lord, what have we done?
What have we done to ourselves, to your creation, to
    you?

We have made our bed in hell; but you are there.
Buying us back and healing the world and offering us
    life again
At the price of Jesus and his cross
And in the power of his mighty resurrection.

Keep us, O Lord, from the things that would destroy
    us.
Keep us seeking after you,
That we may do your will and please you.
Keep us in the paths of righteousness
For your name's sake,
Amen.

Lord Jesus Christ, the crucified
Crying at the last, 'My God why hast thou forsaken
      me?'
And entering the pit.
For us you descended into hell.
So you have kindled hope in hopeless hell
And sown among the damned doubts of damnation.
The cross of Jesus is planted in the depths as it is
      established in the heavens.
So neither the world above nor the world below
Nothing in all creation can separate us from the love of
      God.
O God whose kingdom is everlasting, we offer to you
With the whole Church on earth and in heaven,
Glory, thanksgiving and praise for ever and ever.

Lord Jesus Christ, you have promised
That against your Church the gates of hell shall not
      prevail.
Your Church is surrounded, embattled.
Attacked by great forces of evil in the world
And by greater forces of evil within
Godlessness and materialism attack;
While hypocrisy and carelessness corrupt.
Lord Jesus Christ fulfil your promise
Defend your Church against her enemies
And cleanse her of her sin
That the gates of hell shall not prevail against her.

Lord Jesus Christ, you have promised
That the gates of death shall not overcome your
      Church.
As you burst through from death to life
So may your Church explode
Into real and living faith.
As you came in triumph from death to life
So bring us with those whom you have rescued from
      the grave

Through death to risen life with you
To whom with the Father and the Son and the Holy
      Spirit
Be all glory and honour, now and evermore,
Amen.

(A R C M)

3

Prayers for Bible Sunday (Second in Advent)

The earth shall be filled with the knowledge of God, as
the waters cover the sea. The glory of the Lord shall be
revealed, and all mankind together shall see it; for the
Lord himself has spoken.

Living God, we are here, looking towards your
greatness of which we have heard from the past in
other people's lives; expectantly waiting to experience
the same greatness now, in our own lives.

Let it happen, Lord, even though it may disturb
us, shake us, frighten us: confront us with your
greatness, to challenge and change us and fill us with
new confidence.

Give us living words to make us prophetic and
dreamers in the life of the modern world: for the sake
of Jesus Christ our Lord.

Let us confess our sins to God.

Heavenly Father, in the silence of this holy place
and the silence of our hearts, we now confess our sins
to you; we confess that familiarity has made us careless
in our response to your challenge in the scriptures; we
confess that ignorance has caused us to pervert your
truth, and our resistance to your challenge that we
should love you in our neighbours and serve you in
their needs.

So, Father, now we remember before you, the whole company of heaven, and each other, that we have sinned, in thought, word and deed.

Lord, have mercy upon us:
CHRIST, HAVE MERCY UPON US: LORD, HAVE MERCY UPON US.

God, the Father, God the Son and God the Holy Spirit have mercy upon you, pardon and set you free from your sins and give you time to change your lives.

Prayers of Intercession
Mighty God, when we read of your tremendous power and look at this troubled world, we long to see your power at work to put an end to guilt and suffering.

Give to your Church faith to believe, hope to reach out for and love to make real, the promise we have that all tears will be wiped away; that death, mourning, crying and pain will be brought to an end through the creation of a new heaven and earth.

We pray for those who take no delight in conversation, who stonewall the advances of others, and slow down all communication. We pray for those who let their tongues run away with them in idle gossip, who talk themselves silly, and for all their many words say nothing.

We pray for those who talk to impress, and even to keep others at a distance, by bombarding them with long monologues of prejudice and self-justification, and never stop to listen. We pray for those who use words, not to enlighten, but to conceal the truth, and put off the day of action – lying words, by which they not only fool others but deceive themselves.

Finally, for ourselves we pray: Teach us to seek, as travellers who have lost their way. Teach us to listen, as little children to their parents. Teach us to treasure the words, as lovers blissful at the sound of each other's voices; through Jesus Christ our Lord.

Prayers of Thanksgiving
Father, we not only thank you for the splendour and beauty of this world, set in a majestic universe which speaks to us of dreams to be fulfilled.

We thank you too for the magnificence of your work as we have it in the scriptures; for the great stories and the great men and women through whom your truth was brought to people long ago; through whom your truth still comes if we are attentive. We thank you for men and women of our own times who make the scriptures live for us, and that your work is still alive to keep us calm and sane and strong in the service of the world. We thank you too, for all the men and women of the past who have dreamed dreams and seen visions—some of them known and loved by us who are now with you. Therefore, with angels and archangels and with all the company of heaven, we laud and magnify your glorious name, evermore praising you and saying:
>HOLY, HOLY, HOLY,
>LORD GOD OF HOSTS,
>HEAVEN AND EARTH ARE FULL OF THY GLORY
>GLORY BE TO THEE, O LORD MOST HIGH.
>AMEN.

(T G L)

(ii) **Prayers for Christmas**

4

Prayers for Christmas Eve

O God, though the years be many and long that divide us from the Bethlehem of long ago, yet still his

coming speaks to us and warms our hearts, answers our old questions and makes us ask again—
'Where is he who has been born?
We have seen his star
We have come to worship him.'

O God, though we have come by many hard and testing ways to this most blessed night...some of us with all the marks of life upon us...some of us with tired and weary hearts...and some of us with doubtful caution...yet we come, longing to enter into the spirit of this time, desperate for the great, glad excitement of seeing you, the God of history, become the son of Mary: you, the God of eternity, become the one who shares with us our days and times of night: you, the God of love, become a child among us, a friend and brother of the poor, a Redeemer, and a Prince of peace.

Therefore, with our whole hearts, let us make room for the glory of God in our lives tonight.

Though the years are many that divide us from Bethlehem, God is not caught in the web of stories, songs and messages that surround that little town, but where receptive, hospitable eager souls consent to admit him, the dear Christ enters in.

So may he bless us all this night, and weave around us the timeless robe of joy.

(D O)

5

Confession for the Sunday after Christmas

Unto us a child is born, unto us a son is given.

Let us pray: Most holy God, we confess the failure of our Christmasses. All the waiting, all the excitement; but we have never got it right.

In church we have been too sentimental: we have forgotten the smell of the manger and the tramp of Herod's soldiers; we have been too confident: we have forgotten the risk of incarnation, the vulnerability of a baby, helpless and unrecognised.

At home we have been too impatient; we've grabbed at grown-up toys and quick sensations; in our desperate search for pleasure we have missed joy: the joy of God's glory and men's peace.

In our hearts we have tried to take hold of Christmas and so we have not allowed Christmas to take hold of us. Bring us back, O God our Saviour. Save us, O God; Lord help us now. Though Christmas is passed and still we are not saved, let not your time for us be past. Today if you will hear his voice, harden not your hearts.

O Lord, hear our prayer for the sake of your dear son, in whose words we pray, saying: *Our Father....*

(A R C M)

6

Prayers for Epiphany

Eternal God, we worship you in your greatness,
　　in the universe we cannot comprehend,
　　with the sun and moon and stars
　　which remind us of your distance from us.
And yet we recall that a star led the wise men to Bethlehem, and to your Son; and we're glad that in the birth of Jesus, we see you, stooping, guiding, directing, God with us.

Let us confess our sins to God.

Eternal God, we confess that we've not been faithful to the truth which you have revealed to us. We have seen the star, but have followed with faltering steps. We've come with wise men and shepherds, the great and the humble, to worship; but we're obsessed with our worries, and distracted by our worldliness.

Lord, have mercy upon us:

CHRIST, HAVE MERCY UPON US: LORD, HAVE MERCY UPON US.

God the Father, who commands light to shine in darkness, have mercy upon you, drive out the darkness from your hearts, forgive you your sins and bring you to eternal life: through Jesus Christ our Lord.

Father, we pray for all people who still walk in darkness, for whom your light has shone in the world.

We pray for all who are going through the darkness of mourning, because some light of their lives has been taken away in death; and for men and women suffering the hopelessness of poverty and illness through the failure of the rest of us to share; and for their children, dying in despair and pain before they have tasted any pleasure or known the possibility of hope; the innocents who suffer the consequences of human ambition and greed, like the children who were killed by the order of Herod because the Prince of peace had been born.

Out of our helplessness we pray for all your suffering children; for all men and women with power and authority in the world's affairs; for the Church, which is the servant of your power and love.

Give to all your servants the light of liberating love, and let us see rulers and nations, strong and weak, great and humble, rich and poor, coming with joy and praise to the King of kings.

Let him be light for us now, as he has been and will be, for all time and in eternity, for ever and ever.

Prayers of Thanksgiving
The Lord be with you:
AND WITH THY SPIRIT.
Lift up your hearts:
WE LIFT THEM UP UNTO THE LORD.
Let us give thanks unto the Lord our God:
IT IS MEET AND RIGHT SO TO DO.

Father, it is right to give you thanks and praise, for creating the universe, and making us in your own image. We thank you that when we plunged into the darkness of sin, you didn't abandon us, but sent your Son to be our saviour. In his birth and his life, in his death and resurrection, we see the shining of the one true light, and glimpse a part of your glory.

We thank you that you guided wise men from the east to worship at the Saviour's birth. We thank you for the wisdom of every generation which has been offered in your service, for the light which has been shed on your purpose for us. We thank you for the wise and good, for those who have sought peace in the midst of war, and love in the face of hatred; for those who have enriched our lives by their words and music, their ideas and their deeds. We thank you for those in days gone past, and in our own day who have faithfully followed the Light of the world, witnessing to truth, bringing hope, sharing Christ's love and suffering. Therefore with angels and archangels and with all the company of heaven, we laud and magnify your glorious name, evermore praising you and saying:
HOLY, HOLY, HOLY,
LORD GOD OF HOSTS,
HEAVEN AND EARTH ARE FULL OF THY GLORY.
GLORY BE TO THEE, O LORD MOST HIGH,
AMEN.

(T G L)

7

Service for Candlemas

The Psalmist wrote:

Open to me the gates of righteousness: and I will enter and give thanks to the Lord.

Let us pray:

Almighty Father, with your servant Hannah who prayed silently in her heart for a son, and in due time presented Samuel to you in the Temple, our hearts exult in you, and we rejoice in your salvation.

We remember too, this day, the joy of your servant Simeon whose prayer to see the Lord's Christ was answered when Mary brought her Son to the Temple—so we worship you, loving, listening God. We present our prayers and praises before your presence, drawn to your light, seeking your way; through Jesus Christ our Lord.

Let us confess our sins to God.

Father of all, you have revealed yourself to all who can see in the light of Jesus Christ. You spoke to us in human form so that we could hear and understand you, see and follow you. But we confess that we would rather live in the darkened room of our own wisdom, finding our way by common sense, stumbling along with our own philosophy of life. We have been selfish, wilful and opinionated. In the silence we remember the darkness which sin causes in our own hearts.

Lord, have mercy upon us:

CHRIST, HAVE MERCY UPON US: LORD, HAVE MERCY UPON US.

God the Father, God the Son and God the Holy Spirit have mercy upon you: pardon and deliver you from all your sins, and give you time to amend your lives, through Jesus Christ our Lord.

Collect for the Day
Almighty Father,
whose Son Jesus Christ was presented in the Temple
and acclaimed the glory of Israel
and the light of the nations:
grant that in him we may be presented to you
and in the world may reflect his glory;
through Jesus Christ our Lord.

Prayers of Intercession
Great God, we pray now for the Church and the world
in the name of Jesus Christ, the true light and
foundation stone of every life.

Lord God, your ancient and well-loved people, the
Jews, had at the centre of their national life the
Temple, where your Son was taken, recognised and
made known for who he really was, your love, your
hope, your light and your peace for the world. So we
pray, living, loving God, for the Church in this place.
We pray that your Son may be recognised and known
by all who enter this holy place. May all who come here
leave with a light flowing from within and a sense of
direction and your light guiding their path. We
remember and pray for all who are working for peace
and freedom and justice in this world. Living God,
containing in yourself all the fullness of the universe
and more: from you comes our humanity, our manhood and womanhood, from you we receive the diversity
of gifts which together make human life complete.
Give each of us a due sense of our responsibility to the
rest and make us ready to listen and learn from each
other. Father, the greatest gift you give is that of life,
to all of us. Make us always eager to praise and practice
all that does justice to your holiness and trust in us,
and make us proud to be human, proud to be men and
women rejoicing in the marvellous gifts of body, mind
and spirit, which you have given us, and which are

hallowed by your name. Undergird us with a strength which comes from your son, and may all that we do, say or think be cemented to the living stone of life and love, the word made flesh, Jesus Christ our Lord.

Prayers of Thanksgiving
> The Lord be with you:
> AND WITH THY SPIRIT.
> Lift up your hearts:
> WE LIFT THEM UP UNTO THE LORD.
> Let us give thanks unto the Lord our God:
> IT IS MEET AND RIGHT SO TO DO.

Father of this world and of all worlds, we do well, here and now and at all times and in all places, to give you high praise and hearty thanks for all your goodness to us.

It was your silence which voiced the universe and gave us life, speaking volumes for our guidance: out of the silence of your peace your people's praise emerges, rising in eternal crescendo. We thank you that from that first moment when the stars sang their interstellar hymns, to the discordant babble of Bethlehem—you spoke and are speaking to our world. We thank you too for the persistent faith of Simeon, waiting for the Lord's Messiah to appear and culminating in his faith-filled song of peace and light and hope. We thank you, above all, for your love revealed in Christ: facing the worst we could do, faithful, hopeful, enduring to the end. So it is, with angels and archangels, and with all the company of heaven, we laud and magnify thy glorious name, evermore praising thee and saying:
> HOLY, HOLY, HOLY,
> LORD GOD OF HOSTS,
> HEAVEN AND EARTH ARE FULL OF THY GLORY.
> GLORY BE TO THEE, O LORD MOST HIGH,
> AMEN.

Our Father....

Offertory
Lord God, we come with no great gifts to offer. We are
ordinary folk, some more gifted than others, some
with greater capacity for love, some more in need of
being loved; yet what we have we bring to you to make
your love felt in the loneliness of other people's lives.
    Lighten our darkness, we pray you Lord, and by
your great mercy, defend us and all whom we love,
from all perils and dangers of this night, for the sake
of Jesus Christ, your Son, O Lord.

(T G L)

(iii) **Prayers for Lent and Easter**

8

Prayers for Seventh Sunday before Easter

The Son of man did not come to be served but to serve
    And to give up his life as a ransom for many.

Lord Jesus Christ, you came to serve.
As you came to a blind man and gave him sight
Come to us in our darkness and show us the things we
    cannot see.
As you came to a man tormented in his mind
And gave him peace and healing
Come to us in our tensions and make us whole.
As you came to Lazarus dead and brought him from
        the grave
Come to us in our deadness

And bring us to real life now with our living Lord.

Lord Jesus Christ, you came not to be served but to
       serve
But we see life the other way round:
To get where we do not give
To exploit whom we have not helped
To use what we have not earned.
As you came to a dying thief and promised him
       paradise
Come to us now in forgiveness and hope.

Lord Jesus Christ, you came to serve.
As you came to a friendless tax-gatherer
And gave him purpose and delight
Come to us and renew us with your high calling
That we may love and serve you
Now and for ever,
Amen.

                         (A R C M)

9

Prayers for First Sunday in Lent

Lord God, King of the universe, ruler of all time and
space, you alone are worthy of all the praise of every
person in every age. You dwell in glory beyond our
imagining, in light unapproachable, yet you come to us
in Jesus. We praise and adore you for that mystery.

    Lord Jesus Christ, sharing our humanity, bone of
our bone and flesh of our flesh, to you belongs all
praise imaginable: mild you laid your glory by; a
helpless baby in his mother's arms; taking the form of

a servant; ready for God's call to ministry; sharing baptism with sinners; spending yourself for all who needed you; risking the envy of powerful men; tempted as we are, yet without sin; obedient to death, even the death on the Cross.

Holy Spirit, leading us into all the truth that is in Jesus, to you belongs all the praise imaginable. Through you our lives become a home for the Christ. Father, Son and Holy Spirit we worship and adore you.

Let us confess our sins to God.

Lord, we confess to you what we are.

We like the path of life to be easy, comfortable, untroubled. We like problems to melt away, hardships to be smoothed over, stones to turn into bread for us.

We do not want the hard way that Jesus takes. We like every step to be free from fears. We like to see mighty power helping us at every turn. We like miracles to be happening for our benefit. We do not want the faithful way that Jesus takes.

We like the world to be at our feet, to be lords over our lives, and everyone else's, to be kings of creation, viewing everything from a great height. We do not want the humble way that Jesus takes.

Lord, all the grace of those forty desert days, arm us against those temptations, alert us to their corruption, forgive us our sins. Teach us to tread the way that Jesus takes.

Lord have mercy upon us:

CHRIST, HAVE MERCY UPON US: LORD, HAVE MERCY UPON US.

Almighty God have mercy upon you, pardon and deliver you from all your sins, confirm and strengthen you in all goodness and bring you to eternal life, through Jesus Christ our Lord.

Prayers of Intercession
These prayers are the prayers used by the Taize Community
in France—and at the end of each prayer we say:
REMEMBER YOUR LOVE: O LORD.

Lord, we pray you to inspire continually your Church universal with the Spirit of truth, unity and peace:
REMEMBER YOUR LOVE, O LORD.

Give grace to all bishops and ministers, that by their life and their faith they may show forth your work of truth and celebrate your sacraments in love and in joy:
REMEMBER YOUR LOVE, O LORD.

Give your grace to all your people, and to us met together in your presence; may we hear and receive your word with purity of heart and true obedience, to serve you all the days of our life:
REMEMBER YOUR LOVE, O LORD.

We pray you to give your guidance to all who govern us, disposing their hearts to lead us in peace, according to your will; grant that they may truly seek after justice:
REMEMBER YOUR LOVE, O LORD.

We implore you to help and comfort all who live in trouble, sadness, want or sickness: especially...in praying for them we ask for light and peace for them:
REMEMBER YOUR LOVE, O LORD.

We bless your holy name for all your servants who have passed from this life in faith and in obedience. We pray for grace to follow their example and to share with them in your kingdom:
REMEMBER YOUR LOVE, O LORD.

Prayers of Thanksgiving
Father, it is right for us to give you thanks and praise. Even though you are the God of all eternity, you have not left us to struggle on our own. You have acted so decisively for us in Jesus our Saviour.

We thank you that when we are too hurt to forgive others, you are overflowing with mercy to all; when we are too callous to notice the pain of others, you feel it in yourself; when life bewilders us and we do not know what the good is, you maintain your righteous will; when we are at our weakest, in pain or doubt or distress or self-pity, you know our frailty but remain strong for us; when we want to run away from life, you keep with us and hold resolutely to your purposes of love.

Father, we go into the world, where there are so many wildernesses; where we may starve for affection; where we may experience rejection or neglect; where our stand for your truth and love may be misunderstood or simply not noticed.

But Christ is there before us, crucified and risen. Help us to mount his cross and reach for his resurrection life, finding our greatest joy in doing your will and helping to bring his suffering to its ultimate glorious triumph; so that he, with you, may be praised in the Spirit, without interruption, everywhere and for ever and ever....

(T G L)

10

Palm Sunday: 'Outreach'

'The Church lives by mission as a fire lives by burning' (Emil Brunner).

Leader: Let us draw near to God
All: FOR WHOEVER LIVES IN THE SHELTER OF
            THE MOST HIGH IS SAFE IN THE SHADOW OF
            HIS WINGS:

Leader: Let us bring our lives to God
All: FOR HE CARRIES US DAY BY DAY, HE NEVER
          SLUMBERS AND HE NEVER SLEEPS:
Leader: Let us open our hearts to God
All: FOR HE KNOWS ALL ABOUT US AND HAS
          DISCERNED OUR THOUGHTS FROM AFAR:
Leader: Let us confess our sins to God
All: FOR HE IS COMPASSIONATE AND GRACIOUS,
          SLOW TO ANGER AND ABOUNDING IN
          STEADFAST LOVE.

Call to Prayer and First Prayer

Leader: Jesus said: 'We are now going to Jerusalem,
          and the Son of Man will be given up to the
          chief priests and the doctors of the law; they
          will condemn him to death and hand him
          over to the foreign power'.

          Let us pray: Lord our God, on this day,
          Jesus your Son entered Jerusalem, the centre
          of politics, the capital of religion, the heart of
          the nation's life, for you are the God who is
          always pressing at the centre and striking at
          the heart of things:
All: BLESSINGS ON HIM WHO COMES IN THE
          NAME OF THE LORD
Leader: In the market place, where people buy, and
          sell, and trade,
All: BLESSINGS ON HIM WHO COMES IN THE
          NAME OF THE LORD
Leader: In the board room, where people wheel, and
          deal, and bargain,
All: BLESSINGS ON HIM WHO COMES IN THE
          NAME OF THE LORD
Leader: In the law court, where people probe, and
          debate, and judge,
All: BLESSINGS ON HIM WHO COMES IN THE
          NAME OF THE LORD

Leader: In the school and the college, where people
          teach, and learn, and discuss,
All: BLESSINGS ON HIM WHO COMES IN THE
          NAME OF THE LORD
Leader: In the council chamber, where people argue,
          and plan, and compromise,
All: BLESSINGS ON HIM WHO COMES IN THE
          NAME OF THE LORD
Leader: In the home, where people grow, and share,
          and create,
All: BLESSINGS ON HIM WHO COMES IN THE
          NAME OF THE LORD
Leader: In the Church, where people pray, and
          worship, and betray,
All: BLESSINGS ON HIM WHO COMES IN THE
          NAME OF THE LORD.
          BLESSINGS ON HIM WHO COMES IN THE
          NAME OF THE LORD, FOR YOUR LOVE'S SAKE,
          AMEN.

Second Prayer
Lord, our God,
     You have called us to be the Church, on the move,
travelling light, dying to live, ready to lose ourselves
for the sake of the world.
     You have invited us to be the Church, with a
purpose, sustained by your spirit, united for outreach,
committed to the gospel for the hope of the world.
     And we are the Church, but with a problem—too
strong for the weak, too staid for the young, too
respectable for the poor, too divided for mission, too
much of a reflection of the culture around us, too
unsure of our message to speak to the world.
     Move us from where we are to where you want us
to go: so that we have a sense of your world-wide
communion, and share something of the vitality of the
Church in Africa, the vigour of the Church in Latin

America, the poverty of the Church in India, and the courage of the Church behind the Iron Curtain.

Take us from what we are to what you want us to be, so that we become a community where all are welcomed and no-one is excluded, all are valued and no-one is made to feel inadequate, all are forgiven and no-one is too ashamed to belong, all are encouraged and no-one is too hurt to come among us.

Lead us from who we are to who you want us to be, so that patience is built into us, kindness is assumed in us, gentleness is part of us, compassion flows out from us, truth is second nature to us, no score of wrongs is kept among us, goodness is our everyday pattern, and the commitment of love is binding upon us, through Jesus Christ, our Lord, in whose words we say the prayer that spans the world:

Our Father....

(R F B)

11

A Service of Meditation for Good Friday

Introduction
We meet to remember the death of our Lord Jesus Christ, and to meditate on the mystery and power of his suffering for the sins of the world. Let us pray that we may understand what it means that he died for us; and also that we may receive his Spirit to carry the Cross with him in the world today.

Hymn: We sing the praise.
We shall follow the story of the Death of Jesus as it is told by St John.

First Reading: The betrayal of Jesus by his disciples (John, 18: 1–27).
A period of silence.
A spoken Meditation on the betrayal of Christ by his own people.

Prayer: Almighty God, we give thanks and praise and worship, with your Church in every place and throughout the ages, for the grace that has come to us once for all in our Lord Jesus Christ.

It is with shame and sorrow, as we think of him, that we confess our failures to be his true disciples; we have not followed him in his concern for the poor, the despised and the lost ones; we shrink from being wholly committed to his way of meekness; we long for the prizes that this world can give, and are too easily turned aside from his way of faith and hope and love.

Lord have mercy on us,
Christ have mercy on us,
Lord have mercy on us.

In your forgiving love, most merciful Father, accept our sorrow for our sins, and strengthen us in the resolve to be his disciples indeed, by his Spirit in us, all the days of our life. For his love's sake. AMEN.

Hymn: Alone thou goest.
Second Reading: The trial before Pilate (John 18: 28–19, 16).
A period of silence.
A spoken Meditation on the Kingdom of Christ, the truth he incarnates and his rejection by the world then and now.

Prayer: Almighty God, you have given us a vision, in the word made flesh, of the freedom and fulfilment you have purposed for our human race. May that vision never fade from our minds and wills. May your Spirit be strong to sustain its power against the darkness and evil in our human hearts, and in the world around us.

We pray for men and women unjustly accused; for prisoners of conscience; for children born to poverty; for those rejected because of their race or colour; for innocent victims of violence and war.

Lord Jesus Christ, despised and rejected, Man of Sorrows and acquainted with grief; be present with your brothers and sisters who bear the pain of the world. Strengthen them in spirit. Send them present help and uplift them with the hope of your Kingdom.

Lord hear their prayer. AMEN.

Hymn: O sacred Head, sore wounded.

Third Reading: The Crucifixion (John 19: 17–30).

A period of silence.

A spoken Meditation on the mystery and glory of the Cross: that God was in Christ, reconciling the world to himself.

Prayer: Almighty Father, we are filled with wonder, and awe and reverent worship, as we wait before the Cross that atones for our sins, and proclaims your measureless love for weak and erring men and women. Thanks be to God for his gift beyond words, through Jesus Christ our Lord.

Holy Spirit of God, come to us and move our hard hearts, that we may sorrow with Christ for our torn humanity, and for all homeless souls, and become his body in the world today.

I am persuaded that neither death nor life, nor angels, nor principalities nor powers, nor things present nor things to come, nor height nor depth, nor any other creature, shall be able to separate us from the love of God, in Christ Jesus our Lord. AMEN.

Fourth Reading: The burial of the body of Jesus on the eve of the Sabbath (John 19: 31–42).

A period of silence.

E

Prayer: As the Lord Jesus said, It is finished, so we accept in faith, and in great thankfulness and gladness, his holy life and sacrificial death for us and for our world.

As the Lord Jesus committed himself in dying into the Father's hand, so let us commit ourselves, with all that concerns us, to his infinite power and goodness.

Father, into your hands we commit ourselves and all dear to us, and the world for which we pray.

The Peace of God, that passeth all understanding, keep your hearts and minds in the knowledge of God, and of his Son Jesus Christ our Lord; and the blessing of God Almighty, the Father, the Son and the Holy Spirit, be with you all, now and evermore. AMEN.

(J M)

12

Easter

Thank you, God, for Easter. For the certainties of our faith. For the spirit surging into the Church and its people in their creative and sacrificial lives lived out in Christ.

Thank you God for Easter. For the newness of Spring. For all the lifting expectations of new life available to them who are broken, defeated and killed by the world. Come to them, in the risen power of the Lord Jesus Christ.

Thank you God for Easter. The Great Festival of the Church. The starting place of faith. Let us be filled with the joy of it. Let us sing out from the grace of it. Let us sing out from the love of it. Let us rejoice in the open hope of it. Let your spirit dance through our souls with it. Let your grace cover us like a mantle with it. Let your purity shine within us by it.

Let your forgiveness lift our burden through it. Let your compassions soothe our wounds through it. Let your mercy cover all men and women through it.

That they may know the joy of Christ the Saviour Risen and Exalted bringing forth his Kingdom for all mankind.

We ask it through Jesus Christ our Lord who taught us when we pray to say: *Our Father....*

(K C)

13

An Easter Prayer of Approach and Confession

Eternal God, our heavenly Father, with gladness in our hearts and songs on our lips we come into your house this Easter Day to worship you and to celebrate your mightiest act—the raising of Jesus Christ, from the dead.

Lord Jesus Christ, we rejoice that death could not hold you in its grip, but that you rose again triumphant, greeting your incredulous friends, convincing them that you were the same Jesus who was dead but is alive for evermore; changing their sorrow to joy, giving them new life and new hope.

We too are your friends. Reveal yourself to us now in your risen power, we pray, as we worship and adore you; for you live and reign with the Father in the unity of the Spirit, God for ever and ever....

Let us confess our sins to God.

God our Father, even on this the brightest of all mornings there is still lurking in each one of us a darkness, and so we confess to you, in each other's company and before the whole company of Heaven that we have sinned. We've not always found it easy to recognise your coming to us. Often our spirits are downcast and we, who looked for so much in Christ, are frankly disappointed. Like Simon we denied you in the inmost secret of our hearts. We have denied you with our lips, and yet you have marked our tears and read our thoughts. Read them now, as in the silence we confess how and where and when we have sinned in thought and word and deed and in what we have left undone. . . .

God, who, through the mighty Resurrection of his Son, our Blessed Lord, has wiped out the past, forgive you your sins, give you time to amend your lives and lead you to everlasting life.

The Collect or Prayer for Easter Day:
Lord of all life and power, through the mighty Resurrection of your Son you have overcome the old order of sin and death and have made all things new in him: grant that we, being dead to sin and alive to you in Jesus Christ, may reign with him in glory; to whom with you and the Holy Spirit be praise and honour, glory and might now and in all eternity. Amen.

(T G L)

14

Easter Prayer

If in this life only we have hope in Christ, we are of all men most miserable: but now is Christ risen!

O Lord our God, we give thanks to you for Easter Day:

For the assurance, that Jesus Christ is your Son, and that he is the Saviour of the world, and that all power is given to him.

For the conviction renewed within us that the meaning of our life is found in the Cross and the empty tomb.

For the claim laid anew upon us that Christ is sovereign.

For the hope set before us that victory remains with love.

With the first disciples who with wonder learned that the Lord was risen, we would ascribe glory to you.

With disciples through the ages who, as Easter Day has come, have known afresh that it was all true.

In fellowship with the millions through the world who keep this day with us.

In fellowship with the Church in Heaven, those who have already entered into the fullness of the victory won this day—we give you adoration and praise.

Almighty God, who brought again from the dead our Lord Jesus, grant us this day with fresh eyes to see and with sincere hearts to believe, and with all our souls to confess him our Lord and our God.

Forgive us, O God, who have so often gone our own way, when a living Lord was at hand to lead and guide. Forgive us, O God, who have so often struggled on in our own strength when all the resources of eternity was available to us through Faith.

Forgive us, O God, who have been so slow to believe, so slow to obey.

Forgive us, O God, to have refused the comfort of him who has conquered death, and the daily help of him who has conquered sin.

Forgive us that we have been cast down and dismayed by the changes and chances of this world, when our Saviour Christ has overcome the world.

Speak to our hearts the words that will declare forgiveness for sins past, strength in testing yet to come, and purpose in the days lying before us.

Lord Jesus, stand among us in your risen power and be known to us in your mercy and grace. And to you, who with the Father Everlasting and the Spirit of life now live and reign forever, we shall ascribe all glory on this day and for evermore.

(W J G M)

15

An Easter Prayer of Approach

Adapted from the liturgy of the Russian Orthodox Church

Rich and poor together
let us keep the festival.
Carefully, extravagantly,
let us bring to this moment,
give this moment
a momentous quality.

Let none of us feel overwhelmed
by what is wrong
and out of joint
in the way to live,
for pardon has arisen from the grave.
Let none of us fear death,
for the Saviour's death has redeemed us.
He has destroyed death
by yielding to it.
By entering the land of shadow
he had done away with it.

That land was outraged
by his being there,
for by his being there
he made the shadows lose their dread,
their mystery,
their strangeness.

He confronted them
and they were powerless before him.
The land of Shadows
could not hold him!
Christ is risen
and his victory belongs to us.
Christ is risen
and our fears have lifted from us.
Christ is risen
and life is in his hand,
our hand
our certain grasp.
To Christ be glory
and dominion;
mastery
and possession,
now and forever
century upon century

(D O)

(iv)   **Prayers for Pentecost**

16

Leader: Those who live as their human nature tells
them to, have their minds controlled by what
human nature wants.

All: THOSE WHO LIVE AS THE SPIRIT TELLS THEM TO, HAVE THEIR MINDS CONTROLLED BY WHAT THE SPIRIT WANTS.

Leader: But we do not live as our human nature tells us to: instead we live as the Spirit tells us to, if in fact God's Spirit lives in us.

All: IF THE SPIRIT OF GOD WHO RAISED JESUS FROM DEATH, LIVES IN US, THEN HE WHO RAISED CHRIST FROM DEATH WILL ALSO GIVE LIFE TO OUR MORTAL BODIES, BY THE PRESENCE OF HIS SPIRIT IN US.

Leader: Let us pray: Gracious and ever-loving God from the beginning, you have been so much with us and for us, so mysteriously, invisibly moving through our lives, so deeply, disturbingly, drawing us out of ourselves, so personally, penetratingly present in all our living, that we can only speak of you and address you in the language of persons and in the images of relationships. So you are to us maker, redeemer, lord, and king, shepherd, father, guide, and friend. You gave yourself to us in Jesus your Son, and today we celebrate the gift of your spirit dwelling in us and among us.

All: YOURS IS THE PRAISE AND THE GLORY, THROUGH JESUS CHRIST OUR LORD.

Leader: From the beginning you have been blowing the wind of your spirit through us making us forever dissatisfied without you. Continue now breathing the breath of your life into us, making eyes that are shut open, hearts that are hard tender, hands that are tight unclench, arms that are crossed unfold, minds that are closed aware, bodies that are tense relax, feelings that are cold warm, and lives that are dead live again.

All: GIVE US A NEW HEART AND PUT A NEW
         SPIRIT WITHIN US.

Leader: From the beginning, you have been leading
         us on the road to life, inspiring us towards
         the good of your kingdom. Go on now
         wakening friendship in us for other people,
         and creating joy in us for everything happy
         and human.

All: GIVE US A NEW HEART AND PUT A NEW
         SPIRIT WITHIN US, THROUGH JESUS CHRIST
         OUR LORD, AMEN.

Prayers of Gratitude and Concern
Holy Spirit of God:

Through countless wanderings, you have been our companion, pouring yourself out to make known to us the hidden depths of the eternal's purpose, sustaining our resolve to walk with you on the narrow road to self-giving and service, bearing us up to face in your strength the trials and the sorrows of our human experience, lifting our spirits to celebrate with you the mysterious diversity of life's rich pattern.

You make us responsive to the wonder of creation and the sound of music, the colour of art and the rhythm of words, the power of drama and story.

You make us sensitive to the difficulties of decision-making, the complexities of politics, the temptations of power, the dangers of wealth, and the choices of life and love.

Lead us now to the lonely places where people are accompanied only by their memories and struggle against the resentment of being neglected and un-wanted and forgotten.

Take us now to the hurting places where people seem determined to destroy themselves and have long since given up good feelings about themselves or their reason for living.

Guide us now to the guilty places where people are crippled by a deep sense of shame and carry the pain of an unhappy past that weighs them down and keeps them imprisoned.

Direct those who find themselves in hard places where people are confronted with hard decisions about education and health and transport and jobs and there are no obvious and easy answers.

And in all things, help us to bear one another's burdens and so fulfil the law of Christ, in whose words we pray together saying: *Our Father....*

(R F B)

17

Let all the world praise you this day, Holy Spirit of God, power of the Father come to claim our lives, grace of the Son come to perfect us. Through you comes the energy by which the world is made, the stars are formed, the great galaxies are spread throughout space, the light shines and the darkness is overcome.

Through you comes the fight of life breathed into every human being, so that we belong to the Father and find our peace in him.

Through you comes the visions of the young and the dreams of the old, the strong words of the prophets and the preachers, the joyous songs of the psalmists, the teaching and commands of the Lord. Through you the scriptures bear their witness. Through you comes the life of the Church, the vitality of the faith, the healing of our bodies, minds and spirits. You make your people holy.

Through you comes our confidence for the future, our trust in your full purpose. Glory be to you,

Holy Spirit, Lord and giver of life, from all who were and are and ever shall be. Amen.

Let us confess our sins to God.

Gracious God and Father, on this triumphant and glorious day, burning with fire, red with flames, there are words from your Book which strike us hard: There will be visions and dreams. But we're stuck in our ways, for we've stopped dreaming. The believers were all together in one place, but we're so divided. There were sounds of wind and sight of fire. But we expect nothing to change, nothing new to happen. They spoke with new freedom. But we're tongue-tied, too dumb or too frightened to speak to you.

Father, on the day the Church celebrates her birthday we remember that there's much of which we're ashamed, for we've sinned, in thought and word and deed, and in what we've left undone.

Lord, have mercy upon us.

CHRIST, HAVE MERCY UPON US: LORD, HAVE MERCY UPON US.

God the Father, God the Son and God the Holy Spirit have mercy upon you, pardon and set you free from all your sins and give you time to amend your lives, through Jesus Christ our Lord.

Prayers of Intercession

Father, you have made it clear that the work of your Spirit is not out of this world, but here, where we are, where our fellow human beings go hungry; where war, or fear of war, insensitivity, brutal ambition and selfish greed increase suffering and insecurity, bring us nearer disaster.

Keep disturbing us and give us no rest until we see the world's direction changing. Keep alive in us the vision and dream of universal peace and justice. And in that same dream we pray to you for your Son's Church and its servants, proclaiming your ever-present Spirit: especially today we remember....

In the vision of justice, freedom and dreaming of world peace, we pray that your Holy Spirit will direct and govern the minds of those upon whom is laid the high responsibility of electing members of Parliament for the High Court of Parliament in this realm. We remember again our gracious Sovereign Lady, the Queen, her husband and all the members of her family.

And since we are linked together by the ties of kinship, love and friendship; we remember our families and friends, wherever they may be, those whom we know who are ill at home or in hospital, the sad, those of this community who are perplexed or uncertain of their future....

Father, of your infinite goodness, set us aflame with that fire of the Spirit Christ brought upon the earth and longed to see ablaze, for he lives and reigns with you and the Spirit now and for ever. Amen.

Prayers of Thanksgiving
Father, today, especially, we thank you for your Holy Spirit, sharing in all creation from the very beginning of time and space and matter. We thank you, by whom Mary was chosen: Jesus was born and anointed and filled, he took hold of suffering, facing fairly and squarely death and was glorified: by the same Spirit the Church was born.

We thank you, Holy Spirit of God, for life transformed and made new—for old thoughts giving way to new dreams; old ways giving place to the new life in Christ; old caution giving way to new courage; old fears giving way to new confidence.

We thank you for your new life amongst the first disciples, for Peter and James and John, transformed by you. We thank you for the new life amongst the next followers, in Paul, Barnabas and Timothy. We thank you for the long succession of followers and saints, people like Ninian of Whithorn, Columba of Iona, Mungo of Glasgow, Aylward of China, Schweitzer of Africa, Waite of the Middle East, Roger of Taize in France—all made new by your power. We thank you for those we once knew and loved here on earth who trained us in the faith and called us to new life. So it is, that our voices are joined with theirs, as with angels and archangels and with all the company of heaven, we laud and magnify your glorious name, evermore praising you and saying,

HOLY, HOLY, HOLY,
LORD GOD OF HOSTS,
HEAVEN AND EARTH ARE FULL OF THY GLORY,
GLORY BE TO THEE, O LORD MOST HIGH.
AMEN.

(T G L)

Section III

Sacraments and other Ordinances

(i) *Prayers for Baptism* Page
1 Harris   The Sacrament of Baptism   135
2 Harris   Act of Commitment and
            Welcome to the Table   140
3 Lewis   The Baptism of an Adult Believer 142

(ii) *Prayers for Communion*
4 Brown   (a) Invitation to Communion 145
5 Brown   (b) Invitation to Communion 147
6 Lewis   An Advent Communion   148
7 Harris   An Order for Communion   152
8 Lewis   The Lord's Supper: Feast of the
            Future   156
9 Lewis   A Liturgy of the Incarnation 161
10 Lewis   A Communion Prayer   164

(iii) *Prayers for Marriages*
11 McLellan   Marriage Service   165
12 Forrester   An Order for Marriage   170

(iv) *Prayers for Funerals*
13 W J G McDonald (a) Funeral Prayer   174
14 W J G McDonald (b) Funeral Prayer   176
15 W J G McDonald (c) Funeral Prayer   177
16 W J G McDonald (d) Funeral Prayer   178
17 W J G McDonald (e) Funeral Prayer   179
18 Wylie   Memorial Prayer   179

Sacraments and other Ordinances

(i) Prayers for Baptism

1

The Sacrament of Baptism

Whether baptism be of a child or an adult, the sacrament demands action by the faithful Church. The congregation's part is not one of witnessing merely, but of direct involvement in their faithful actions throughout the service.

In each case the service is the culmination of a process of preparation in which those asking baptism for themselves or for their child, together with the congregation, carefully consider the responsibilities which baptism holds for them.

No difference is seen between adult and infant coming to baptism, this being God's act effected by the Spirit, and by the Church in dependence on the Spirit. In infant baptism, the parent's confession is seen as a witness to the child's place in the covenant.

The first response to the baptism that has taken place is surely that of the Christian community, receiving, welcoming, and pledging responsible care for its new member. In the case of a child, the parent takes a twofold part in this: as member of the fellowship and as special minister to the child within the fellowship, and the fellowship has a direct responsibility to further this ministry. In the case of an adult, commitment starts with baptism, and is not a precondition of baptism.

Much of the service is common to both infant and adult baptism. Where there are differences, the parallel sections are set side by side.

We receive and welcome A and B who by appointment of the Kirk Session bring their child to be baptised today.

We receive and welcome N, who, having been under instruction, is commended to you by the Kirk Session, and by their appointment now presents her/himself to be baptised, and to commit her/himself to Christ.

Hymn:

Brothers and sisters in Christ, let us prepare ourselves to act as his Church, recalling the meaning of baptism and our responsibility in it. Indeed the Spirit of the Lord is upon us, for by grace Christ Jesus, having died and risen for all humankind, has baptised us into his new life, made us part of his Body, and given us his Spirit. And he calls us to accept and to care for all whom he chooses to bring into his Body; for it is in this Body, made alive by the Spirit, that they will grow in him.

By baptism Christ makes us one with himself, and one with each other in him. It is in this faith that we baptise in the name of the Father and the Son and the Holy Spirit, and take our share of responsibility for each new member so added to Christ's Body and Church universal.

Therefore let us pray for God's help:

Lord, strengthen our faith in our baptism, and help us by your Spirit as we act in your name. Make us yet more aware that we are one with you and with each other in your Body, that all who are joined to it may grow in grace: through Jesus Christ our Lord.

Let us stand and declare the faith of the Church:
I BELIEVE....

A and B, as the Church

N ..., as the Church we

we are commanded in faith to seek out and to baptise those whom Christ evidently takes to himself—among them, those who by his grace are children of faithful members of his body. Therefore we ask you:

Do you believe in one God, Father, Son and Holy Spirit; and do you confess that Jesus Christ is Lord and trust him as your Saviour?

I DO

What then hinders your child to be baptised? For the promise is to you, and to your children, and to everyone the Lord our God may call.

are commanded in faith to seek out and baptise those whom Christ evidently takes to himself. The sign of this for you and for us, is that by his grace you have come to have faith in him. Therefore we ask you:

Do you believe in one God, Father, Son and Holy Spirit and do you confess that Jesus Christ is Lord, and trust him as your Saviour?

I DO

What then hinders you to be baptised? For the promise is to you, and to everyone the Lord our God may call.

Let us pray the Spirit to act with us:

Lord God, with joy we thank you for N .... As we baptise with water, baptise her/him with your Holy Spirit, that born again and set in Christ's Body (s)he may live by your power in newness of life; through our Lord Jesus Christ.

N ..., by command of our Lord Jesus Christ we baptise you in the name of the Father and the Son and the Holy Spirit.

Welcome, child/sister/brother in Christ!

THE LORD BLESS YOU AND KEEP YOU...

Let us pledge ourselves to take up the responsibilities this baptism lays upon us:

Do you, Christ's people here pledge yourselves and his Church to love and to care for this new member of his Church universal?

WE DO

A and B, do you her/his parents pledge yourselves with God's help to bring her/him up to know Christ through your love and care, and to teach her/him that (s)he is a member of the Church?

WE DO

Do you, Christ's people here, pledge all fellowship and help to these parents in their task?
—WE DO

Jesus said: If anyone declares publicly that he belongs to me, I will do the same for him before my Father in heaven.

N..., may our Lord's commitment to you help you to commit yourself to him. May he be with you as you speak truly from your heart:

Do you commit yourself to follow Christ, to serve him with all your heart and strength and mind, and to take your full part in the life and work of his Church universal?

I DO, ASKING HIM TO HELP ME. (*Hands are laid upon the candidate.*)

Lord, by your Spirit bless and strengthen N..., that (s)he may keep this most solemn promise and be faithful to you to the end.

In the name of the Lord Jesus Christ, King and Head of the Church, we

welcome you to your place
at his table and your part
in his work; and together
in his presence we say to
you:

WE PLEDGE OURSELVES
TO YOU IN THE
FELLOWSHIP OF HIS
BODY, FOR THOUGH WE
ARE MANY WE ARE ONE IN
HIM, BECAUSE WE ALL
SHARE HIS ONE BREAD.

In the name of this
congregation and the
whole Church universal
we give you the right
hand of fellowship....

The following or other suitable prayers are offered:
Lord, in whose baptism we are made one with you and
with each other, keep us ever faithful in your body,
serving and loving one another in the Spirit, that the
world may know and believe in you, to whom, Father,
Son, and Holy Spirit, the one eternal God, be glory in
the Church for ever.
      Let us bless each other:
      THE GRACE OF THE LORD JESUS CHRIST
      AND THE LOVE OF GOD
      AND THE FELLOWSHIP OF THE HOLY SPIRIT
      BE WITH US ALL EVERMORE.
      AMEN.

(S H)

2

Act of Commitment and Welcome to the Table

The Session Clerk or other representative reports:
I have to report on behalf of the Kirk Session that we
have found that those persons I am about to call
forward have come to understand the meaning of their
baptism, and want to commit themselves to fullness of
life in the Church. They have been under special
instruction, and we believe that their desire is sincere.
We therefore call upon them to profess their faith and
commitment publicly, and to hear us as we in turn
commit ourselves to them.

Will you please come forward as I call your
name....

The minister addresses them:
Brothers and sisters, in your baptism our Lord joined
you to his Body, and made you members of his
Church. Now we rejoice that by his grace you have
come to understand this, and have decided to acknowledge it, to declare your faith in him, to commit
yourselves to him, to join us at his table, and to share
in his work in the world.

Therefore let us pray:
Lord Jesus, head of the Church,
by your Spirit you have joined us to yourself
in your baptism of death and resurrection.
Help us to die to the old and rise to new life in
you.
Help us to realise the unity you have given us
together in your Body,
that the world may see your saving love.
Let us stand and declare the faith of the Church:
I BELIEVE....

Jesus said: If anyone declares publicly that he belongs to me, I will do the same for him before my Father in heaven.

N..., may our Lord's commitment to you help you to commit yourself to him. May he be with you as you speak truly from your heart:

Do you believe in one God, Father, Son and Holy Spirit, and do you confess that Jesus Christ is Lord, and trust him as your Saviour?

I DO

Do you commit yourself to follow Christ, to serve him with all your heart and strength and mind, and to take your full part in the life and work of his Church universal?

I DO, ASKING HIM TO HELP ME.

Hands are laid on each candidate:
Lord, by your Spirit bless and strengthen N... that (s)he may keep this most solemn promise and be faithful to you to the end.

In the name of the Lord Jesus Christ, King and Head of the Church, we welcome you to your place at his table and your part of his work; and together in his presence we say to you:

WE PLEDGE OURSELVES TO YOU
IN THE FELLOWSHIP OF HIS BODY,
FOR THOUGH WE ARE MANY
WE ARE ONE IN HIM,
BECAUSE WE ALL SHARE HIS ONE BREAD.

In the name of this congregation and the whole Church universal we give you the right hand of fellowship....

THE LORD BLESS YOU AND KEEP YOU....

Let us pray:
Father, we rejoice that you have brought us to this hour. Now build us all up in the unity of faith and love, that in what we are and what we do the world

may know our Lord Jesus Christ, to whom with you
and the Holy Spirit be glory for ever.
Let us bless each other:
THE GRACE OF THE LORD JESUS CHRIST
AND THE LOVE OF GOD
AND THE FELLOWSHIP OF THE HOLY SPIRIT
BE WITH US ALL EVERMORE.
AMEN.

(S H)

3

The Baptism of an Adult Believer

Just as the Body is one and has many members, and all
the members of the Body, though many, are one Body,
so it is with Christ. For by one Spirit we were all
baptised into one Body, Jews or Greeks, slaves or
free—and all were made to drink of the one Spirit.
Let us pray:
Lord our God, we gather united as one Body in
the freedom and exhilaration of your gospel, with our
eyes upon the Cross of Christ your Son. We celebrate
and praise him—united in flesh with our humanity;
identified in water with our sin; cursed in godforsaken-
ness with our death; raised in glory for our re-creation.
Here we rejoice with sign and song, in memory
and in expectation. We proclaim humanity's deliver-
ance from the floods of evil and destruction; her
exodus emancipation from all that frightens and
enslaves. We remember our own rebirth from old to
new existence, cleansed from the pride and sloth and
self-protectiveness which stains in us your image of
self-giving love. We anticipate in vision and dramatic

action the crumbling of every human barrier—the walls of race and nation, class and sex which postpone your final kingdom of freedom, unity and love; for whose coming we pray together now: *Our Father....*

Readings: Matthew 3:13–17, Matthew 28:16–20, Romans 6:1–4, Galatians 3:27–29.

N...: it was for you that Jesus Christ was born, in the weakness of your flesh he struggled and was tempted; for your sins he died; in your grave he lay; with your body he was raised; in your redeemed humanity he sits at God's right hand, making you a forgiven, cherished daughter in the Triune family of love.

So, N..., I baptise you in the name of the Father...

and of the Son...

and of the Holy Spirit. Amen.

The Lord bless you and keep you; the Lord make his face to shine upon you and be gracious to you; the Lord lift up his countenance upon you and give you peace. Amen.

N...: having thus received the sign of a salvation and a calling which are already yours, do you publicly confess your faith, and do you promise to consider yourself dead to sin and alive to God in Christ Jesus, placing all your hope in him, and trusting in the power of his Spirit?

I DO.

As a baptised member of the Body of our Lord, the communion of his saints, do you promise to live in the fellowship of faith, where we bear one another's burdens, speak the truth in love, and grow up into Christ who is our head?

I DO.

Called to share in Christ's ministry and mission to the world, do you promise to live a life of daily baptism and of faithful witness to the reconciling of humanity and the coming of God's rule?

I DO.

Sisters and brothers: If you have remembered your baptisms, have heard again the good news of Christ crucified, and are willing to confess afresh your faith in his forgiving love and reconsecrate your lives to his costly discipleship, will you respond WE DO to these questions:

Do you remember that while you were yet sinners Christ died for you, give thanks for every sign and recollection of your burial with him, and promise to walk for the rest of your days in the newness of his resurrection life?

As baptised members of the Church of Jesus Christ, do you pledge yourselves anew to all your partners in the household of faith; and do you promise in particular to support your sister N..., with your prayers, encouragement and love?

Along with her and all Christ's servants everywhere, do you promise to persevere in our Lord's commission, to take the gospel into all the world, baptising disciples and witnessing by word and deed to his victory over darkness, sin and death?

There is one Lord, one faith, one baptism; so let us enact our old but reappropriated unity, by greeting our sister with a handshake, or a holy hug.

Let us pray:

Lord our God, we dare not close this act of joy and celebration without a moment of sorrow and repentance. We have seen and heard and dramatised the oneness of humanity, the promise that in baptism there is no longer Jew or Greek, slave or free, male or female. We have thus participated in a lie; for your Church is not one, still less your world. The thrill of our fellowship and unity, our liberating knowledge of forgiveness, our victory celebrations over death, would be hypocrisy did we not bring into this moment and into this circle the sounds of violence, the smells of disease, the sights of poverty, the passions of guilt and hate and fear, everything which mocks faith's vision of salvation. You do marvellous things with us; yet in honesty your kingdom seems far distant, your future remote from the reality of our still divided selves, our disunited churches, our disordered world. Let our sacramental sign of your future kingdom, and our sense of the presence with us of him who makes all things new, constitute not only our protest against the status quo, but our commitment so to love you and serve our fellow human beings, that the new creation, when tears and death shall be no more, will become a vision of reality for many more as it has come alive for us (tonight) in hope and thankfulness and joy.

(A L)

(ii) **Prayers For Communion**

4

(a) **Invitation to Communion**

Leader: All through the gospels, there are stories about Jesus meeting with all kinds of different people. Some have names that are part of our history—Zacchaeus, the superintendent of taxes, Bartimaeus, the blind man in Jericho, Lazarus, the brother of Mary and Martha, Nicodemus, the member of the Jewish Council, and the madman mid the tombs whose name was Legion.

The names of others are unknown, but

their stories are equally familiar—the son of the widow at Nain, the epileptic boy at the foot of the mountain, the man with the withered arm in the synagogue, the deaf mute in the territory of the ten towns, and the woman of the streets living an immoral life.

Like us, some of them were sick, some were guilty, some were dead, some were half-alive, and some were on the road to self-destruction. To all, Jesus offered newness of life, and the invitation to health, wholeness and well-being.

This offer and this invitation are still made to all who see the great love of God revealed in Jesus the Son.

At this table, all are welcome who believe that here we can find the things that make for our peace, and the nourishment to help us live as God intends.

All: JESUS SAID: I AM THE BREAD OF LIFE.
WHOEVER COMES TO ME SHALL NEVER BE HUNGRY,
WHOEVER BELIEVES IN ME SHALL NEVER BE THIRSTY,
WHOEVER COMES TO ME I WILL NEVER TURN AWAY,
FOR I HAVE COME THAT YOU MAY HAVE LIFE IN ALL ITS FULLNESS.

Leader: Let us draw near to God
All: FOR HE WISHES TO DRAW NEAR TO US.
Leader: Let us open up our hearts to God
All: FOR HE STANDS AT THE DOOR AND KNOCKS.
Leader: Let us taste and see that God is good
All: FOR HIS PROMISES NEVER FAIL.

(R F B)

5

(b) **Invitation to Communion**

In St John's gospel, there's a story telling us that Jesus went to Jerusalem for one of the Jewish Festivals. He came to the Sheep Pool in Jerusalem, where, among the colonnades, there lay a crowd of handicapped people, some lame, some blind, some paralysed. Among them was a man who had been crippled for 38 years.

When Jesus saw the man lying there, he asked him a seemingly strange question: 'Do you want to recover?' And the man said: 'Well, I've no-one to put me in the pool when the water is disturbed, and while I'm moving, someone gets there before me'. And Jesus replied: 'Rise to your feet, take up your bed and walk.'

Many of us are here today because we want to recover, from past guilt, mistakes and failures that may have haunted us for many, many years; from a present sense of inadequacy that has left us now lacking in self confidence; from an acute loss of faith that has led us to doubt everything and believe nothing; from a hard, personal experience, like bereavement, that has made us cold, numb and insecure.

Many of us are here today because we want to recover our strength, our sense of moral balance, a proper understanding of human relationships, and a true perspective on life's meaning and purpose.

To all of us, Jesus extends an invitation—to rise up and walk with him, and in his company find the strength and the confidence to be the whole, integrated, faithful people God means us to be, and so be able to live as God intends us to live.

We come, not because we are strong, but because we are weak; not because any goodness of our own gives us the right to come, but because we need mercy and help. We come, because we love God a little and would like to love him better. We come, because he loves us and gave himself for us.

(R F B)

6

An Advent Communion

Call to Worship
In many and various ways God spoke of old to our fathers by the prophets. But in these last days he has spoken to us by a Son. For since God's children share in flesh and blood, he himself likewise partook of the same nature, as one who in every respect has been tempted as we are, yet without sin. Let us then with confidence draw near to the throne of grace, that we may receive mercy and find grace to help in time of need.

Let us pray:
Eternal Lord, God of Abraham, of David and of Mary, and Father of Jesus Christ Immanuel, we worship you with joy and trepidation. We have gathered to remember the Messiah's coming among us in transient flesh; to look for his coming again in translucent glory; and to encounter his coming now in gospel word and graphic sign. Yet every time and manner of his coming disturbs us with its demands no less than it excites us with its promises. Because of its costliness we would prefer to postpone and flee away from the advent of your grace; because of its bounty and freeness, we reach out for your grace hungrily and urgently, exposing our wounds of body, mind and spirit to your

healing light, and the frayed and tired sinews of our fellowship to the integrating, energising power of your love.

Heal and reconstitute us as one body now, united.

Invitation to the Table
Mary sang of the God who does great things; who came to fill the hungry with good things. Christ Jesus, son of Mary, son of God, says this:

I am the living bread which came down from heaven; if any one eats of this bread, he will live for ever; and the bread which I shall give for the life of the world is my flesh.

This is the Lord's Table, and he welcomes all who hunger and thirst, all who weep and are wounded. His flesh is food indeed; his blood is drink indeed; and in his kingdom there shall be no more tears and no more pain.

The Declaration of Oneness:
THE CUP OF BLESSING...
The Sign of Peace:
Let us express our communion with our neighbours, with the handshake, hug or kiss of peace.
The Call to the Spirit:
Let us call upon the Spirit together...

The Prayer of Thanksgiving
Lord our God, we lift up our hearts to you in glad thanksgiving, joining our voices with all the company of saints and angels, to adore your holiness and acknowledge that heaven and earth are full of your glory. You make all things—the seeds in our soil, the stars in our sky, the scenery in our city. And you have made us, in your own image. From the cells in our bodies, to the thoughts in our minds, to the passions in our hearts, we are persons like you, created for

fellowship and reciprocity as your children and friends. We are stunned to hear, and we struggle to comprehend, that in your Son the Word has become flesh, the Creator a creature, the Lord a servant. For your Advent Yes to creation and to all humanity, we praise you. For your Good Friday No to all the evil, sin and death that disfigures creation, destroys life and dehumanises us, we worship you. We give you thanks for the living reminders set before us now, of flesh assumed, flesh broken, flesh raised, transfigured, healed. Grant us as we eat and drink, new faith in Christ's incarnate presence; new love for Christ's Calvary passion; new hope through Christ's Easter promise. In whose name we pray. Amen.

And now, our intercession for humanity:

Leader: Christ Jesus, Son of the Father, child of Mary, who had come in human flesh, we pray for all whose integrity and worth as human beings is under threat: the unborn victim of irresponsibility and folly; the child abused by violence, neglect, and exploitation; the confused adolescent and the bitter youth; the adult under strain, the disappointed middle-aged, the discarded elderly.

All: COME, IMMANUEL, REASSURE THEM WITH YOUR PRESENCE

Leader: Christ Jesus, Lamb of God, Saviour of the world, who died in human flesh, made sin for us. We acknowledge our complicity in human wickedness; and we pray for the victims of oppression and of war, of prejudice and inequality; and for those who having suffered much bring suffering to others in their anger and confusion.

All: COME, IMMANUEL, REDEEM THEM BY YOUR GRACE

Leader: Christ Jesus, Risen Lord, Ascended King,
who has been exalted in human flesh, and
sits beside the Father clothed in our humanity.
We pray for those who through loneliness or
bereavement, disease or handicap, feel that
they are incomplete and only half alive; and
for all minorities excluded from full mem-
bership of your family in the Church or in
the world, or banished to the margins of
society.

All: COME, IMMANUEL, RESTORE THEM TO YOUR
WHOLENESS.

And we pray as Jesus himself taught us: Our Father...

The Breaking of Bread:
On the night of his betrayal, Jesus took bread and
when he had blessed and given thanks he broke it and
said: This is my body which is for you; do this in
memory of me.

In the same way he took the cup (*take*) and said:
This cup is God's new covenant, sealed with my blood;
whenever you drink it, do so in memory of me.

This means that every time you eat this bread and
drink from this cup, you proclaim the Lord's death
until he comes.

The Sharing of the Meal:
Take, eat, this is the body of Christ which is
broken for you. This do in memory of him. The blood
of Christ, shed for you.

The Dismissal to the World:
Sisters and brothers: This celebration of the
incarnation is not ended. It has only just begun. Go
now into the world to proclaim Messiah's advent. With
word and song, deed and prayer, flesh out the good
news for men and women everywhere, that God
himself is with them and among them, made flesh for
them and their salvation.

F

Let us say the Grace together: The grace of our Lord Jesus Christ, the love of God and the fellowship of the Holy Spirit, be with us now and forever more. Amen.

(A L)

7

An Order for Communion

This is so set out that, if desired, the leading may be shared by two or three people, with the minister as president, and the parts in CAPITALS may be said by all.

The Approach
Hymn: This is the Lord's table, not ours. We therefore will rejoice if members of any branch of his Church share this holy meal with us. For we, with his whole Kirk, are his body here on earth; and in sharing this meal we are joined to him and to each other in him.

Clearly we cannot truly share it if we are holding anything against each other. Nor can we meet our Lord without remembering our shortcomings, and admitting those things of which we are ashamed. Yet he knows us for what we are. In grace he accepts us; in love he invites us to be open with him; in mercy he forgives us, even before we ask.

Let us pray:
Lord, be with us at your table.
COME, LORD JESUS!
Lord, make us open to you.
The Lord says: Here I stand knocking at the door: if anyone hears me and opens the door, I will come in and sit down to supper with him, and he with me.

Lord, we are afraid to open ourselves to you, to open ourselves to others. Only by meeting you can we change.

COME, LORD JESUS!

Meet us here, meet us in each other, meet us in the very needs of the world.

COME, LORD JESUS!

Meet us in our hearts, where we're ashamed of things we've done, of things we've shirked, of hurts we've given, of forgiveness we've refused to give.

COME, LORD JESUS!

Make us so conscious of you as to know that you lift this load from us, in your merciful love. Set us free to live as you want us to live. Amen.

By grace we are forgiven;

By grace we are set free through our Lord Jesus Christ.

THANKS BE TO GOD!

The peace of the Lord be always with you:

AND ALSO WITH YOU.

In his peace, let us give each other the right hand of fellowship....

The service continues with ministry of the Word
The offering

Let us make our offering...

Let us pray:

Lord, you give us yourself:

Teach us to give in the freedom you have given us.

We bring this money:

Put it to use, with all our offerings, for the folk of our parish and the world.

ACCEPT IT, LORD

Remembering our commitment to you, we offer ourselves:

Help us to do it freely.

ACCEPT US, WE HUMBLY ASK.

Remembering our commitment, we offer ourselves to each other:

HELP US TO ACCEPT EACH OTHER AS YOU ACCEPT US:

FOR THOUGH WE ARE MANY, WE ARE ONE BODY, BECAUSE WE ALL SHARE IN ONE BREAD.
AMEN.

The Act of Communion
Hymn: Let us pray:

Lord we come, not trusting in ourselves but only in your dear Son, our strength and Saviour. Amen.

The Lord Jesus said: I am the bread of life. Whoever comes to me shall never be hungry, and whoever believes in me shall never thirst. He who comes to me I will never turn away.

And he gives us his actual self: for on the night in which he was arrested he took bread and after giving thanks to God, broke it and said: This is my Body, which is for you: do this, that I may be remembered. In the same way he tok the cup after supper and said: This cup is the new covenant sealed by my blood: whenever you drink it, do this that I may be remembered.

CHRIST HAS DIED, CHRIST IS RISEN, CHRIST WILL COME AGAIN.

Dearest Lord Jesus, make yourself known to us in this breaking of bread. Amen

As Jesus took bread and a cup, we take this bread and wine: and as he thanked God, let us do the same:

HOLY, HOLY, HOLY LORD,

GOD OF POWER AND MIGHT:

HEAVEN AND EARTH ARE FULL OF YOUR GLORY:

HOSANNA IN THE HIGHEST!

Lord God, you loved the world so much that you gave your only Son, that everyone who has faith in him may have eternal life.

With joy and thankfulness we remember him, in whom we have life, in whom we are one. We praise and thank you for his coming, for what he said and did, for his death on a cross and his rising from death in victory; and we thank you for the Spirit he sends us, for the love he bears us, for the sure hope of his coming again.

Thus remembering our Saviour's work, we make this memorial of him before you until he comes again. And we pray you so to move us by this Spirit that this bread we break may be a means of sharing in his Body and this cup we drink, a means of sharing in his blood, that we by faith may be made bone of his bone, flesh of his flesh, one with him and with each other in him, that the world may know and know him in us and be served by him through us.

Lord, we have faith:

Help us where faith falls short.

Our Father....

Remember Jesus, who took bread and broke it...and said: This is my body, which is for you.

Remember Jesus, who took the cup...and said: This cup is the new covenant, sealed by my blood.

Lamb of God,

You take away the sin of the world:

Have mercy on us.

LAMB OF GOD,

YOU TAKE AWAY THE SIN OF THE WORLD:

HAVE MERCY ON US.

LAMB OF GOD,

YOU TAKE AWAY THE SIN OF THE WORLD:

GIVE US YOUR PEACE.

Take this, and eat:

This is his Body, which is for you.

The bread is shared:

Drink of this, all of you: for this is his blood of the covenant, shed for all for the forgiveness of sins.

The cup is shared:
The peace of Jesus be yours always.
AND YOURS AS WELL.
Father, with all our heart we rejoice that we and all who believe in Christ our Lord are made one in him. We give thanks for this fellowship, and for those who have gone before us in this faith, who though they are dead are alive for ever in Christ Jesus. Keep us loyal to him, so caring about all people that we may share life in his body now, and his splendour hereafter.
Here intercessions may be made.
Now may the God of peace make of us what he would have us be, through our Lord Jesus Christ, to whom with the Father and the Spirit be glory for ever. Amen.

Hymn: The peace of God, which is beyond our utmost understanding, keep guard over our hearts and our thoughts, in Christ Jesus. Amen.
Let us join hands ... and bless each other as we go, saying:
THE GRACE OF THE LORD JESUS CHRIST
AND THE LOVE OF GOD
AND THE FELLOWSHIP IN THE HOLY SPIRIT
BE WITH YOU ALWAYS.
AMEN.

(S H)

8

The Lord's Supper: Feast of the Future

The Invitation to the Feast
A Hymn of the Feast:
The Feast Promised

Leader: This day shall be a memorial day: you shall keep it as a feast to the Lord through every generation.

All: IT IS THE PASSOVER OF THE LORD. HE FREES HIS PEOPLE AND BRINGS THEM TO A LAND OF MILK AND HONEY.

Leader: At twilight you shall eat flesh, and in the morning you shall be filled with bread: then you shall know that I am the Lord your God.

All: YOU PREPARE A TABLE BEFORE ME IN THE PRESENCE OF MY ENEMIES; YOU ANOINT MY HEAD WITH OIL, MY CUP OVERFLOWS.

Leader: The Lord of hosts will make for all peoples a feast of fat things, a feast of wine on the lees, of fat things full of marrow.

All: IT WILL BE SAID ON THAT DAY: LO, THIS IS OUR GOD; WE HAVE WAITED FOR HIM, THAT HE MIGHT SAVE US. LET US BE GLAD AND REJOICE IN HIS SALVATION.

Leader: He shall feed his flock like a shepherd.

All: YEA, HOW GOOD AND HOW FAIR IT SHALL BE! GRAIN SHALL MAKE THE YOUNG MEN FLOURISH, AND NEW WINE THE MAIDENS.

The Feast Inaugurated

Leader: Jesus said: Your fathers ate manna in the wilderness; but I am the living bread which came down from heaven; those who eat of it will live for ever.

All: YOU ARE THE BREAD OF LIFE. FEED US THAT WE MAY NEVER HUNGER. GIVE US TO DRINK THAT WE MAY NEVER THIRST AGAIN.

Leader: Jesus said: Can the wedding guests fast while the bridegroom is with them? As long as they have the bridegroom with them, they cannot fast.

All:　　　WE THANK YOU, LORD JESUS, THAT YOU
　　　　　EAT AT TABLE WITH TAX-COLLECTORS AND
　　　　　SINNERS.

Leader:　Jesus said: When you give a feast, invite the
　　　　　poor and the maimed, the lame and the
　　　　　blind.

All:　　　HE GAVE THEM LOAVES AND FISHES, AND
　　　　　ALL OF THEM WERE SATISFIED.

Leader:　Jesus said: I have food of which you do not
　　　　　know. My food is to do the will of him who
　　　　　sent me. Remove this cup from me; never-
　　　　　theless, not my will.

All:　　　WE REMEMBER HIS DEATH; WE FEED UPON
　　　　　HIS LIVING SACRIFICE.

Leader:　The Lord Jesus on the night he was betrayed
　　　　　took bread, and when he had given thanks,
　　　　　he broke it, and said: This is my body which
　　　　　is for you. Do this in remembrance of me. In
　　　　　the same way also the cup, after supper,
　　　　　saying: This cup is the new covenant in my
　　　　　blood. Do this as often as you drink it, in
　　　　　remembrance of me.

All:　　　AS OFTEN AS WE EAT THIS BREAD AND
　　　　　DRINK THIS CUP, WE PROCLAIM THE LORD'S
　　　　　DEATH UNTIL HE COMES.

The Feast Consummated

Leader:　Jesus said: I shall not drink again of this fruit
　　　　　of the vine until that day when I drink it new
　　　　　with you in my Father's kingdom.

All:　　　WOMEN AND MEN WILL COME FROM EAST
　　　　　AND WEST AND NORTH AND SOUTH, AND SIT
　　　　　AT TABLE IN THE KINGDOM OF GOD.

Leader:　Lift up your heads, O gates! and be lifted up,
　　　　　O everlasting doors! that the King of glory
　　　　　may come in.

All: NOW WE SEE IN A MIRROR DARKLY BUT THEN WE SHALL SEE FACE TO FACE.

Leader: God himself will dwell with us and we will be his people. He will wipe away every tear from our eyes, and there will be no more death, no more crying or pain.

All: BLESSED ARE YOU THAT WEEP NOW, FOR YOU SHALL LAUGH.

Leader: Those who sow in tears shall reap with shouts of joy!

All: TO THE THIRSTY HE WILL GIVE FROM THE FOUNTAIN OF THE WATER OF LIFE, WITHOUT PAYMENT.

Leader: Holy, Holy, Holy is the Lord God Almighty!

All: WHO WAS AND IS AND IS TO COME.

Leader: Blessed is he who comes in the name of the Lord.

All: COME, LORD JESUS, QUICKLY COME!

Leader: The kingdom of the world has become the Kingdom of our Lord and of his Christ.

All: And he shall reign for ever and ever!

The Invitation

Sisters and brothers, grace to you and peace from God our Father and the Lord Jesus Christ. God invites all those who love the Lord to feast at this messianic banquet. This is the Supper of the New Age, the meal of heaven, our tearful-joyful celebration today of God's tomorrow. Accept God's invitation to the feast, and acclaim the coming victory of Christ.

The Feast Celebrated

The Festive Greeting: Let us greet each other in the peace and love of the reign of Jesus Christ.

    The Call to the Spirit of the Feast: The cup of blessing which we bless, is it not participation in the blood of

Christ? The bread which we break is it not partici-pation in the Body of Christ? Because there is one bread we who are many are one Body, for we all partake of the one bread. And by one Spirit we were all baptised into one Body—Jews or Greeks, slaves or free—and all were made to drink of one Spirit.

And thus, as one community, members of the one Body of Jesus Christ, and baptised by the one Spirit, we together take this bread and wine, and call upon the Spirit of Christ to descend upon us, be among us, and raise us up to heaven, that *this* may be for us the bread of life, and *this* the cup of our salvation. In the eating and drinking, and in the sharing, may the incarnate Christ be born again in our hearts, the Crucified Christ remembered, the Risen Christ acclaimed, the Returning Christ greeted already with joy.

United thus in love and expectation, let us pray together as Jesus taught us, to his Father and our Father...

The Festive Sharing: On the night of his betrayal... (*Communion*)

Sisters and brothers: Salvation belongs to our God, who sits upon the throne, and to the Lamb that was slain. From every creature in heaven and earth, be blessing and glory and honour and thanksgiving! For ever and ever. Amen.

The Feast Extended

Go in peace. Live as free men and women. Serve the Lord. Rejoice in the power of the Spirit. And be glad that the Kingdom of God is coming.

(A L)

9

A Liturgy of the Incarnation

'When the time had fully come, God sent forth his Son, born of woman.'

Incarnation announced:

Leader: Ephesians 2: 14–15

All: FOR THE BREAKING DOWN OF EVERY BARRIER IN CHRIST'S OWN FLESH, WE GIVE YOU THANKS AND PRAISE. FORGIVE THE BARRIERS OF RACE AND NATIONALITY, OF CULTURE AND OF CHURCH, WHICH TEAR APART CHRIST'S FLESH ANEW. USE OUR GIFTS THAT THE UNITY AND PEACE OF CHRIST MAY BE REALISED IN OUR DIVIDED LAND AND THROUGHOUT THE WHOLE WIDE WORLD.

Leader: Matthew 1: 20–23

All: FOR THE CREATIVE POWER OF YOUR SPIRIT, WHO MAKES ALL THINGS, AND MAKES ALL THINGS ANEW, WE GIVE YOU THANKS AND PRAISE. BY THE CREATION OF YOUR SPIRIT YOUR SON HAS COME AMONG US, IMMANUEL, GOD WITH US, BORN TO SAVE US FROM OUR SINS. THROUGH THE SPIRIT'S GIFTS OF FAITH AND HOPE AND LOVE, MAY WE OURSELVES BE RECREATED, TO WALK IN CHRIST'S NEW LIFE AND TO REFLECT HIS LIGHT.

Leader: Luke 1: 34–38

All: FOR THE OBEDIENCE OF MARY, OUR SISTER IN THE FAITH, WHO LET IT BE TO HER ACCORDING TO YOUR WORD, WE GIVE YOU THANKS AND PRAISE. IN HUMILITY OF SPIRIT AND SACRIFICE OF BODY, MAY WE TODAY LET CHRIST BE FORMED ANEW IN US, AND HIS ABUNDANT LIFE BE THE FRUIT OF OUR

OBEDIENCE. SO MAY THE TALENTS OF EACH WOMAN AND THE GIFTS OF EVERY MAN FIND FULL EXPRESSION IN YOUR CHURCH, AND IN YOUR WORLD.

Leader: Romans 8: 3–4

All: FOR THE PRESENCE OF YOUR SON IN THE DEPTH OF OUR CONDITION, HIS SUBMISSION TO THE WEIGHT OF HUMAN SIN, WE GIVE YOU THANKS AND PRAISE. BY HIS LIFE AND DEATH IN OUR OWN FLESH, WE HAVE BEEN SET FREE FROM LAW AND GUILT AND FEAR. KEEP US WALKING ACCORDING TO YOUR SPIRIT, WITH THE LAUGHTER OF THE LIBE-RATED, FORGIVING AS WE HAVE BEEN FOR-GIVEN, LOVING AS WE HAVE FIRST BEEN LOVED.

Leader: John 1: 14–18

All: FOR YOUR ETERNAL WORD BY WHOM THE WORLD WAS MADE, NOW BECOME OUR BROTHER IN THE WORLD, WE GIVE YOU THANKS AND PRAISE. IN HIS FACE WE HAVE PERCEIVED YOUR UNSEEN GLORY; IN HIS WORDS WE HAVE HEARD YOUR UNUTTER-ABLE TRUTH. YOUR SON'S PRESENCE IN OUR FLESH SEALS YOUR COMMITMENT TO ALL CREATION. HE RESTORES TO DIGNITY AND FREEDOM THE HUMANITY OF ALL YOUR CHILDREN. MAY HIS TRUTH AND LOVE BE ENFLESHED AMONG OURSELVES, IN A FELLOW-SHIP OF COMMON FAITH AND MUTUAL RESPECT, AND IN SERVICE TO EVERY NEIGH-BOUR WHOSE HUMANITY IS TRAMPLED AND DENIED. FOR YOUR SON'S SAKE, AMEN.

Incarnation explored:
  The Ministry of Word
  Address

Incarnation celebrated:
    The Ministry of Sign and Song
    Hymn
    The Invitation to the Table

The Declaration of Oneness:
All: AS ONE COMMUNITY, MEMBERS OF THE ONE
            BODY OF CHRIST, AND BAPTISED BY THE
            ONE SPIRIT, WE TAKE THIS BREAD AND
            WINE. WE CALL UPON THE SPIRIT OF CHRIST
            TO DESCEND ON US, BE AMONG US AND
            RAISE US UP TO HEAVEN. MAY THIS FOOD BE
            FOR US THE BREAD OF LIFE, AND THIS DRINK
            THE CUP OF OUR SALVATION. IN THE EATING
            AND DRINKING AND IN THE SHARING, MAY
            THE INCARNATE CHRIST BE BORN AGAIN IN
            OUR HEARTS, THE CRUCIFIED CHRIST RE-
            MEMBERED, THE RISEN CHRIST ACCLAIMED,
            THE RETURNING CHRIST GREETED WITH
            JOY.

The Prayer of Thanksgiving

The Intercession for Humanity:
Leader: Christ Jesus, Son of the Father...
All: COME, IMMANUEL, REASSURE THEM WITH
            YOUR PRESENCE.
Leader: Christ Jesus, Lamb of God...
All: COME, IMMANUEL, REDEEM THEM BY YOUR
            GRACE.
Leader: Christ Jesus, Risen Lord...
All: COME, IMMANUEL, RESTORE THEM TO YOUR
            WHOLENESS.

The Breaking of the Bread
The Sharing of the Meal
The Dismissal, to the World
The Saying of the Grace

(A L)

10

A Communion Prayer

Lord our God, we lift up our hearts to you in praise
and thanksgiving, full of wonder and adoration.

In fellowship with all who have trusted you in
every age and every place, we praise your holiness; for
heaven and earth are full of your glory.

We thank you for the love of Jesus Christ, who
came among us to stand where we stand, flesh of our
flesh; that he was no stranger to our darkest night or
to our deepest sorrow; but that on the cross he knew
the weight of guilt, the pain of death, the hell of
separation.

We thank you that the crucified one was raised
again, that from his death comes life, from his
judgement comes forgiveness, from his forsakenness
comes the promise that we shall never be forsaken.

We thank you that the Spirit of the crucified and
risen Christ is at work in our world, bringing light into
its dark corners and already establishing your coming
kingdom of peace and love and justice.

Amid all that causes us and our fellows pain and
fear and doubt, we live by the Spirit of hope, looking
for the redemption of our humanity and the reconciling of all your creatures.

In the Spirit's name we intercede now for all who

need your love. In the quietness we reach out, concentrating our thoughts not upon ourselves, but others.

We reach out to the people sitting beside us at this moment....

We reach out further to all those special persons in our lives whom we cherish and love deeply....

We reach out further still to that network of friends, acquaintances and public figures—whose names we know, but whose real needs we can scarcely understand....

We reach out finally to all those throughout the world, whom *you* know and love, though *we* cannot name them....At all these levels of our relationships we make our intercessions; and we pray that wherever there is need, poverty, oppression, sickness, loneliness or death, women and men may know your healing touch and do your reconciling truth.

And now we pray that the Spirit of joy and thankfulness may be poured out upon ourselves too, and upon this bread and wine, uniting us in the communion of the body and blood of Jesus Christ, in whose name we pray. Amen.

(A L)

(iii) **Prayers for Marriages**

11

Marriage Service

If the Lord does not build the house, the work of the builders is useless.

We are here to take our part in the marriage of A and B.

Let us worship God.

Hymn

Marriage is the simplest kind of human sharing. It is God's means of providing for a man and a woman to live together in love, joy and trust and for enabling children to be brought up in the strength of a happy home. So it has a special place in the Bible and in Christian tradition. In the Bible's own words:

'Marriage is to be honoured by all.'

Each of you has a child of God placed in your hands today. After today forgiveness, loyalty and trust have a new meaning. God's promise is that he will bind you together in your marriage with his love.

Let us pray:

Almighty God our Father, your love has always been at the centre. In Jesus Christ you have offered to us a life of love. We give thanks for the love which has surrounded A and B since the day they were born in their family homes. We praise you for the love which has brought them here today and with them we rejoice that from today their love will be strengthened and sustained by your gift of marriage.

Give them the strength to keep the promises they are about to make, the love which will make them want to keep them, and the courage to grow from these promises ever nearer to one another. Through Jesus Christ our Lord. Amen.

In the Old Testament we read a story which expresses the truth that God meant men and women for each other:

Then the Lord God said—'It is not good for the man to live alone. I will make a suitable companion to help him...'.

Then the Lord God made the man fall into a deep sleep, and while he was sleeping, he took out one of the man's ribs and closed up the flesh. He formed a woman out of the rib and brought her to him. Then the man said, 'At last, here is one of my own kind— bone taken from my bone, and flesh from my flesh. "Woman" is her name because she was taken out of man'. That is why a man leaves his father and mother and is united with his wife, and they become one.

In the New Testament we read of Jesus using that same story to underline his own high view of marriage.

'Haven't you read the scripture that says that in the beginning the Creator made people male and female? And God said, "For this reason a man will leave his father and mother and unite with his wife, and the two will become one". So they are no longer two, but one. Man must not separate, then, what God has joined together.'

Will you stand.

As a seal to the promises you are going to make, give each other your right hand.

A and B you have come together according to God's wonderful plan for creation. Now, before these people, say your vows to each other.

I, A, take you, B, to be my wife. I promise, with God's help, to be your faithful husband, to love and serve you as Christ commands, as long as we both shall live.

I, B, take you, A, to be my husband. I promise, with God's help, to be your faithful wife, to love and serve you as Christ commands, as long as we both shall live.

As a sign of this bond, this ring is given and received. By this sign you take each other to have and to hold from this day forward; for better, for worse; for richer, for poorer; in sickness and in health; to love and to cherish.

In the light of the love that led you here and of the promises you have made to one another before

God, I declare you to be husband and wife: in the name of the Father and of the Son and of the Holy Spirit. Amen.

Will you kneel.

God the Father, God the Son, God the Holy Spirit, bless, preserve and keep you. The Lord pour out the riches of his grace upon you, that you may please him, and live together in holy love until your lives' end. Amen.

Will you stand: and will you be seated.

Marriage is about love. Hear again the Word of God.

Love is patient and kind; it is not jealous or conceited or proud; love is not ill-mannered or selfish or irritable; love does not keep a record of wrongs; love is not happy with evil, but is happy with the truth. Love never gives up; and its faith, hope and patience never fail. Love is eternal.... These three remain: faith, hope and love; and the greatest of these is love. Put love first.

(1 Corinthians 13:4, 13; 14:1)

You must try to be like God, for you are his children and he loves you. Your life must be lived in love, and must have as its pattern the life of Christ, who loved us and gave himself for us, as a sacrifice and offering acceptable to God....

Each one of you husbands must love his wife as he loves himself, and every wife must respect her husband.

(Ephesians 5: 1,2,33)

No one has ever seen God, but if we love one another, God lives in union with us and his love is made perfect in us.

God is love, and whoever lives in love lives in union with God and God lives in union with him.... There is no fear in love, perfect love drives out all fear....

We love because God first loved us.... The command that Christ has given us is this: whoever loves God must love his brother also.

(1 John 4)

The Lord bless to us the reading of his holy Word, and to his name be glory and praise.

Take this book and upon its wisdom build your home.

Let us pray:

Lord our God, we ask for your life-long blessing on A and B. Strengthen their love, deepen their joy in one another, and keep ever fresh in their hearts the promises they have made today. Give them a home filled with warmth and tenderness and brightness, a home in which children may be surrounded by wisdom and affection, a home rooted and grounded in you. Guard them and keep them, keep them faithful to each other and to you until their lives' end, so that they may grow ever more deeply and wonderfully together in the faith and love of our Lord Jesus Christ.

In his words we pray, saying, '*Our Father...*'. Amen.

Hymn

May the Lord bless you and protect you.

May the Lord smile on you and show you his favour.

May the Lord befriend you and prosper you.

The grace of the Lord Jesus Christ, the love of God, and the company of the Holy Spirit be with you all. Amen.

(A R C M)

12

An Order for Marriage

This Order was developed in discussion with a couple who were very uncertain about the specifics of Christian faith but had a general belief in God and a vital experience of love. They wished their marriage to be marked by participation, celebration and honesty. The Order was adapted for various other couples and is printed here as an indication of the kind of thing that may be done.

The bride and groom come up into the church and stand at the kneeler, facing the minister, the bride at the groom's left hand.

Minister: Except the Lord build the house, they labour in vain that build it. Our help is in the name of the Lord, who made heaven and earth.

Hymn

Statement

A: We would like to welcome you and thank you all for coming to participate with us in our marriage ceremony.

B: Special thanks to our parents, families and relations for the love and support you have given us. Thanks to you all, friends, for the hours of work and leisure we have enjoyed with you.

A: Through you and with you all we have come to celebrate our love in this ceremony which marks the beginning of our new life together.

B: We welcome the permanence of our commitment to one another, as providing a basis of mutual trust, friendship and security.

A: We hope this deeper understanding and appreciation of one another will equip us well to work in our chosen fields and enrich our contract with the world.

B: We look forward to creating and supporting our own family.

A: We hope our home will be a place where people will come to talk of joys and sorrows.

Minister: I welcome you, A and B, and your families and friends to this House of God and I am happy to take part with you in this ceremony of marriage because I believe that God is love, that it is he who has brought you together, and that his grace is at work deepening your love and understanding of each other and binding you closely and joyfully to each other. I believe that marriage is an institution pleasing to God because it enriches his children and human society. You have come publicly to affirm that you will love, cherish, support, encourage, and comfort each other as long as you live. I am here to proclaim God's blessing on your relationship, a blessing no less permanent and reliable than the vows you will shortly take.

Prayer: For the many paths and experiences through which you have brought us all to this place and to this moment we praise you, O Lord. Most of all we are moved and glad for the coming together of A and B in trust and love. Enrich with your grace at this hour their highest ambitions and deepest hopes. As we celebrate their love and joy and their dedication to each other and to the service of others, bless us all with peace and happiness.

Let sincerity and affection be in all that is said and done, so that this service may be a true act of worship.

You are blessed, O Lord our God, King of the universe, Creator of all. You are blessed, O Lord, who make bridegroom and bride to rejoice. You are blessed, O Lord our God, King of the universe, who have created joy and gladness, bridegroom and bride, mirth and exaltation, pleasure and delight, love, brotherhood, peace and fellowship. You are blessed, O Lord, who make the bridegroom to rejoice with the bride.

Silence
The Lord's Prayer

The Vows
A: I, A take you, B to be my lawful wedded wife, to have and to hold, from this day forward, for better, for worse, for richer, for poorer, in sickness and in health, to love, honour, and cherish, as long as we both shall live, according to God's holy ordinance.
B: I, B take you, A to be my lawful wedded husband, to have and to hold, from this day forward, for better, for worse, for richer, for poorer, in sickness and in health, to love, honour and cherish, as long as we both shall live, according to God's holy ordinance.

The ring is given to the Minister, who says:

Bless, O Lord, this ring, that he who gives it and she who wears it may abide in your peace, continue in your favour, live, go on, and grow old in your love; through Jesus Christ our Lord. Amen.

The ring is returned to the groom who places it on the bride's finger.

Minister: You have heard A and B as they have covenanted together in this place and before this congregation. I declare them to be husband and wife, in the name of God the Father, God the Son, and God the Holy Spirit. I remind you of the words of Jesus Christ: A man shall leave his father and mother and be made one with his wife; and the two shall become one flesh.... Those whom God has joined together, must not be separated.

Couple kneel

May the Lord bless and protect you, may the Lord smile on you and give you favour; may the Lord be glad in you and grant you peace. Amen.

Couple sit
Reading 1: *eg* 1 Corinthians 13, 4–8 and 13
Reading 2: *eg* 1 John 4, 7–11
Address
Prayer: (*kneel*)
Father, you have given to humankind the ordinance of marriage and hallow it with your blessing: Bless, we pray, your children A and B, and grant that, bearing one another's burdens, sharing one another's joys, and together fulfilling the duties of home and society, they may always be faithful to each other in love and gaiety. Be present with them to enrich and deepen their commitment, care and understanding, and make their home a place where the celebration of this moment

continues and flowers down the years: through him who shared in Nazareth the life of an earthly home. Amen.

The grace of the Lord Jesus Christ, the love of God, and the fellowship of the Holy Spirit be with us all. Amen.

Hymn
The signing of the Register
Procession out

(D F)

(iv) Prayers for Funerals

13

(a) Funeral Prayer

Eternal God, Father of us all, we offer thanks for many things, but especially today for family life and what that has meant in the experience of many of us...for those who have sustained it and given it meaning—for all the challenges and tensions and disciplines of family life, and its sacrifices...all of love that has come to us thereby, and of mutual support, and those in whom we have seen the costliness of it and the rewards of it. And so today for X we give thanks.

We offer thanks for the life of business and of daily work...for those whose commitment and loyalty to that, and whose skill and dedication and responsibility and particular gifts of discrimination and sensitivity have been used to the full. And so too today for X we give thanks.

We offer thanks for the width of human experience

...for all the many-faceted glimpses of human life that we have shared with others who knew more than we did...who enlarged our own dimension as they shared with us what they had seen and found. And so too today for X we give thanks.

We offer thanks for friendship...for those who shared so much with us, without whom our lives would have been impoverished and less colourful and less fulfilled...those whose wisdom and freshness of thought and vitality of spirit, whose profound values undergirding their living, gave a measure of direction to our own living that we would not otherwise have known...and so too today for X we give thanks.

All the happy memories that will abide in cheerful reminiscence when the sadness of this day has passed. And that (s)he was spared too long a twilight...and that at the end he was in caring hands when most he needed them...and that he knew to the end the love and concern of those dearest to him...and the faith that sustained him into the fullness of which he has now come. And that now he sees and understands those things which are yet beyond our understanding, who do not understand the mystery of our coming or of our going hence. Guide and sustain us through the days of our pilgrimage, whether they be long or short, and bring us too at the last through the merits of Christ to the father's house, that we too may hear the words, 'Well done, good and faithful servant, enter thou into the joy of thy Lord'—and that we too, in the company again of those whom we love and for a time have lost, may understand the mystery and may behold the vision glorious, through Jesus Christ, our Lord.

(W J G M)

14

(b) **Funeral Prayer**

Eternal God, we believe that all truth derives from you...and that all knowledge has its source, and its end in you. We whose vision is limited, and whose knowledge is partial, wait now upon you...for we stand in the presence of the ultimate realities...where knowledge falls short, and in our frailty we lean as children upon a father.

We give thanks for the quest for truth which is nothing less than the quest for you. For deceit and falseness and error cannot live in your presence...to know you is to know the truth and to seek for the truth is to seek for you. We give thanks for those who have set their faces steadfastly towards the light and who have walked by the light that they have received... who were determined to follow the truth wherever it should lead...and who have dedicated their gifts to causes greater than themselves.

We give thanks for men and women of intellectual integrity, and for those who have displayed the old-fashioned virtues of honour, and industry, and commitment, who by their lives have challenged us to seek and to follow the narrow way that leads to knowledge and to life itself. Those who have widened the frontiers of knowledge and encouraged others to attempt more than otherwise they should have dared to do.

And so give thanks for our friend X. Some of us because he was a colleague, a fellow pilgrim towards a common goal. Some of us because he taught us much, gave us confidence, gave us freely of his time and because we could trust him and know his loyalty was absolute. And some here because they had known his love...as husband, father, brother and as a very dear friend.

We remember those whose lives are most impoverished by his sudden going from us, because they were the most enriched by what he was and what he gave to them; and recognising in the security and happiness of his home, and the understanding and support of those near to him that provided the foundation upon which alone his life's work could be built, we would the rest of us surround X and Y and Z with our love and concern, in the knowledge of their sorrow and their pride, and rejoicing with them in what cannot ever be taken from them...in love, and example, and memory.

(W J G M)

15

(c) **Funeral Prayer**

Father, we offer thanks for the many people who have been your agents to each of us, who have shared with us their joys and their sorrows, their kindness, their faith, and their love; whose wisdom has instructed our ignorance, whose experience has guided our uncertainty, whose charity has rebuked our intolerance, whose warmth has kindled again our coldness, whose zeal has inspired our lethargy, whose encouragement has enabled us to do more than we thought we could do; those in whose Christian life Faith has been revealed as winsome and gracious and lovely; those who have made the Christian life a credible and desirable thing.

(W J G M)

16

(d) **Funeral Prayer**

We give thanks for X. For his life and for his (her) memory. And we remember not the cutting short of his life with his promise unfulfilled, but rather that life itself, and all that he achieved in it... individually we give thanks for private memories, tender, joyful, to be the more cherished now, and some too deep for tears. Help us to remember, all the good and happy memories that will abide when the pain of this day has passed. Give us grace not to be haunted by the might-have-beens, but to be grateful for what has been, and to find our strengthening in what has yet to be... to believe that neither death nor life, neither things present nor things to come, can ever separate us or those that we love from thy love in Jesus Christ, our Lord. That as he abides for ever in our love, so he abides forever in thine. And for the mystery of eternal life, the world beyond in which all things are made plain... in which wounds are healed, in which the great questions are resolved, the irreconcilables reconciled... in which all things are made new and young again... in which mercy and grace and love are the great realities.

Father God, who hast set our feet upon our own pilgrimage through life, and who knowest how we see the way sometimes and lose it at others, how we fall sometimes and stumble often... guide us on the perilous way that we take... that we may yet reach the goal... for thou hast given us the Way and the Truth and the Life in the life and words and power of Jesus Christ.

(W J G M)

17

(e) **Funeral Prayer**

Eternal God in whose sight our lives are lived, we are indebted to thee for life itself, our tenure of it and our understanding of its meaning and purpose. From thee we came, thy call we return... from eternity to eternity we are with thee.

We bless thee, Lord, for all that enables us to pass our days with confidence and with hope, knowing that there awaits us not the last darkness, but the light of thy glory and the sight of thy face. Especially for thy Word, which gives us promises that only a loving Father could make and an all-powerful God could fulfil. And for thy Son who for us overcame the sharpness of death, and drew the sting of it forever and made it not the end of the road but a gateway to life eternal.

(W J G M)

18

Memorial Prayer

Thanks be to God that memory can be a golden chain; that for all the sorrow there can be reflections of times shared with laughter, and good humour, and goodwill that has made life richer. We pray that for those whose homes, and hearts, know an emptiness, that time may do its healing work; that best memories can be cherished, and that bitterness may be overtaken by the certainty of your love which endures all things.

If our memories are short—forgive us. So inspire us that we can learn positively from the past and reflect honour for all who died by the unity of our continuing fellowship and the respect with which we treat all who share all parts of our lives.

MAY WE RETURN TO THE DUTIES WHICH AWAIT US IN THE WORLD, RESOLVED TO BE MORE FAITHFUL TO YOU, AND MORE HELPFUL TO ONE ANOTHER, FOR THE SAKE OF THOSE NO LONGER WITH US, AND THEIR NEAREST AND DEAREST ON EARTH. THROUGH JESUS CHRIST OUR LORD WE ASK THIS. AMEN.

(W A W)

Section IV

Acts of Worship for Special Services

(i)	*Affirmation of Faith and Commitment*		*Page*
1	Barbour	An Act of Thanksgiving, Penitence and Trust	183
2	Ogston	A Morning Meditation on the Lord's Prayer	185
3	Ogston	'I am'	186
4	A McDonald	Prayer for a Service of Re-dedication	188
5	Winning	An Act of Re-dedication	189
6	Doig	Prayer for the Dedication of Pew Bibles	190

(ii)	*Prayers for Occasional Services*		
7	McLellan	Prayer for a New Year	191
8	A McDonald	Offering Prayer at the New Year	192
9	A McDonald	Prayers for a New Year	193
10	Brown	Prayers for Corrymeela Sunday	195
11	Campbell	Amnesty	198
12	Gordon	Meditation on Remembrance	199
13	Winning	Remembrance	203
14	Longmuir	Remembrance	204
15	McLellan	Prayers for Remembrance Sunday	207
16	Ogston	Prayer for an End of Term Assembly	210

(iii)	*Prayers for Peace, Justice and Healing*		
17	Galloway	A Prayer for Peace	211
18	Galloway	Prayers for Peace and Justice	212
19	Galloway	Prayers for Healing	218
20	Ogston	The Drum Sermon	221

(iv)   *Prayers for Informal, Small Group and Family Worship*

21 Doig	Prayers for a Family Service	223
22 McLellan	An Act of Worship for House Groups	225
23 McIver	Informal Service of Praise and Personal Ministry	227
24 Gordon	A Litany for a Home Communion	230
25 Ogston	A Silver Wedding Anniversary Prayer	232
26 Shaw	(a) Prayer at Start of Meeting	233
27 Shaw	(b) Prayer at Start of Meeting	233
28 Shaw	(c) Prayer at Start of Meeting	234
29 Shaw	(a) Prayer at Start of Kirk Session	234
30 Shaw	(b) Prayer at Start of Kirk Session	235
31 Winning	Grace before Meal	235

Acts of Worship for Special Services

(i) Affirmation of Faith and Commitment

1

An Act of Thanksgiving, Penitence and Trust

When your hand was laid upon us at our baptism, our parents and friends trusted you to fulfil the promises you made to us: and so now
> WE TRUST YOU, LORD

When the first glimmerings of your love and your purpose in Christ came to us, we trusted you, Lord: so now also,
> WE TRUST YOU, LORD

We trust too in our families, our fellow-workers and our friends; through them and because of them
> WE TRUST YOU, LORD

In all our doings, in moments of seeming achievement and moments of seeming failure, whatever our thoughts, whatever our faith or lack of it, we know that
> WE TRUST YOU, LORD

In your apparent absences, at times when you hide your face, in the dark night of our soul, in disillusionment and weariness, because we can do nothing else
> WE TRUST YOU, LORD

At times of our obedience, at all times of our devotion and hard work, when folk speak well of us and praise sings sweetly in our ears; at such times
> WE TRUST YOU, LORD

When we have lost our way, and are drowned in self-importance or the sense of being wronged; despite ourselves
WE TRUST YOU, LORD
And yet we know that all too often we do not trust in you. We trust in our own abilities, our skill or cleverness, our power or craftiness, our ability to cope, our position and our reputation, all that justifies us:

And we fail and we try, we try and we fail, and yet
WE TRUST YOU, LORD
And the miracle is this:
at all times of our obedience and at all times of our disobedience:
in our humility and in our pride:
in our successes and in our failures:
through thick and thin:
for better, for worse:
in sickness and in health
YOU TRUST US, LORD
Without hesitation and without remorse:
Without preconditions and without guarantees:
No deposits paid, no sureties asked for:
YOU TRUST US, LORD
In our loneliness and in our fear:
In our little wilderness, at our little Gethsemanes:
YOU TRUST US, LORD
Whatever we do, wherever we go, whoever we are
YOU TRUST US, LORD
Because you have called us, because you have taken us, because you can't leave us, because we are yours: for today, for tomorrow, for ever
YOU TRUST US, LORD
And shall we not trust you—for today, for tomorrow, for ever?

(R A S B)

2

A Morning Meditation on the Lord's Prayer

God of the pulse of life, God of the vastness of the star-clusters, our Father in heaven...
HALLOWED BE YOUR NAME
Slow as a tiny seed that grows in secret, or obvious and marvellous...
MAY YOUR KINGDOM COME
We do desire, not superficially, but counting what the cost may be, that your will be done...
IN EARTH AS IT IS IN HEAVEN
Lord, we exult in this morning which awakens us to have beginnings...
GIVE US THIS DAY OUR DAILY BREAD
We confess our sin: for living cautiously, for insincerity, for frozen attitudes...
LORD, FORGIVE US
For living without concern for others
LORD, FORGIVE US
For consenting to oppression and all kinds of wrong, both open and disguised
LORD, FORGIVE US
As we forgive those who have failed us
AND LEAD US NOT INTO TEMPTATION
But deliver us from evil. For yours is the Kingdom, yours is the power, and yours is the glory, always.
Amen.

(D O)

3

'I am'

You leave a great space around you, Lord, when you tell us your name.

You leave yourself room to grow, room for amazement, room for the lost dimension of our wonder.

You reserve the right to surprise us.

I AM

I SHALL BE

Lord, in our lust for certitude, in our desire to pin you down, we had expected something more specific: something unequivocal. But you resist us here, as you resist us always, just when we long for the tidy definition, and all the loose ends tied up.

Therefore we enter the broad space around you, which we call worship: and therefore we unleash our minds and unfetter our imaginations, and this we shall describe as prayer—to have the good fortune to be there when the bush flares with flame: to have the honesty to be afraid and nervous about it all: to have the humanity to ask you, 'What is your name? Who are you?'

I AM

I SHALL BE

We praise you, God, for you are the way beyond, the way through, the truth of what is true, the life that lives in us. You are the silence and the voice.

Therefore, we pray, teach us, in our encounters
the time to speak and the time to listen;
the time to interrupt and the time to wait;
the time to play safe and the time to take risks;
the time to be serious and the time to be flippant;
the time to forget ourselves and the time to let our
    own needs come to the surface;

the time for laughter and the time for mute
    accepting sharing of desolation.
Teach us that our language has to be like you—
like your name
    I AM
    I SHALL BE
    a language which is fluid, and expressive of
motion, flexibility and grace.
Lord God,
    we look for a way
    a voice
    an attitude
    with which we may approach you and give the
        glory to you.
With Easter faith
    we speak your gracious name.
With longing and embarrassment
    we confess our sins.
We confess
    to God Almighty,
    to all the company of heaven
    and to each other
    that we have sinned exceedingly in various ways—
    in clever, calculating ways,
    in dull, pedestrian ways,
    in our thinking and in the imagery of our minds,
    in our speech and in the hollowness of our words,
    in our actions and in the selfishness with which we
        pour our energies into the maintenance of
        that kingdom where we are king.
Therefore we ask Almighty God to pity us and to give
us room to turn again to him.
    LORD, HAVE MERCY UPON US
    CHRIST, HAVE MERCY UPON US
    LORD, HAVE MERCY UPON US
    Gracious God, whose friendship we dare not
underestimate, whose love we cannot lightly walk away

from, grant us your pardon, spelled out in glowing colours.

Forgive our sins and cast them into the oblivion they deserve.

Through the risen Christ invade our thinking, our speaking and our doing, that love may be the atmosphere we live in, flourish in and stretch the muscles of our faith in, for Jesus Christ's sake. Amen.

(D O)

4

Prayer for a Service of Re-dedication

'Thank you Lord'

These are the first words that come to mind when we come before you in prayer. Above *all* else, thank you for Jesus; for his life in Nazareth as a carpenter, for his life 'on the road' as a preacher, a teacher and a healer; for his agonising, humiliating death on the cross and his rising from the dead three days later. For all of that we can only say 'thank you'.

We have come today to a special service, to be in communion with you and your word made flesh and our brothers and sisters in Christ throughout this land and this world. And so it is a time for re-commitment and re-dedication, but always remembering Jesus, who was committed and dedicated to us long before we ever knew his name....

We come today, remembering times when we felt very close to God, but believing that God has never been far from us, in our spiritual 'highs' or our grief and despair.

We come today, remembering times when we found prayer easy, but believing that, when we are uninspired, the Holy Spirit prays for us to God, with sighs too deep for words.

We come, remembering days when the bible readings seemed to be speaking directly to us, but believing that the same word of God can still speak to us when we feel distracted, disinterested and dull.

We come, remembering a time when it seemed urgent and important to us every week to set aside part of our money for Christ's Church, but believing that God will always provide our daily bread....

And we come, remembering a time in our lives when we felt our faith could move tenement blocks, but believing that God had faith in us from the day we were created and will continue to believe in us, to forgive us, and to inspire us, until the day we die—which is not a day to fear, thanks to Jesus.... Lord, hear us in the silence as we make our own prayer of rededication....

Short silence.

And now Lord, help us to go and live as free and forgiven people, for Jesus' sake. Amen.

(A M)

5

An Act of Re-dedication

Three unlit candles placed at front of chancel, and one lit in silence after each affirmation. The first could be lit by a member of a uniformed organisation or similar group; the second by a married couple; and the third by the most recent member or youngest baptised child present.

To the congregation, standing, the minister says:
Remembering promises made to individuals, and especially those made in marriage, let us now, depending on the grace of God to help us, affirm anew our intention to keep these promises.

Remembering promises made to God, especially in baptism and on profession of faith, let us now, depending on God's grace to help us, affirm anew our sincere desire and intention to keep these promises.

Let us pray:
O Lord our God, accept us now as we pledge ourselves and all that you have given us, once more to your service.

We have heard your call: Follow me; and we come in obedience and love.

Go before us into our homes, our work, our leisure and the work of your Church; and grant that in these places we may find you, our Companion, our Head and our Lord.

Give us grace to keep true to you and to the promises we have made in our hearts and affirmed with our lips, so that at the last we may enter into the joy of our Lord, even Jesus Christ, your Son, our Saviour, in whose name we ask it. Amen.

(A W)

6

Prayer for the Dedication of Pew Bibles

Here is wisdom. This is the Royal Law.
These are the lively oracles of God.
This is daily bread.
Let me receive it,

O God, you have never left yourself without a witness, we give thanks for your word in every generation.

For this Book that brings us into the presence of your glory, that introduces us to Jesus Christ your Son, that unites the Church in every denomination, in every land and in every language to the glory of your name, we give thanks.

Receive these Bibles that now we present and dedicate, that they may be vision to those who open them, food to those who read and preparation for that abundant life in Christ that is and that is to be.

Hear this our prayer in Jesus' name. Amen.

(A B D)

(ii) **Prayers for Occasional Services**

7

Prayer for a New Year

The Lord is good; his love is eternal and his faithfulness lasts forever.

New year; new hopes; new problems; new resolutions; same old us. With all our old customs for a new beginning for a new year, the new man in us looks very much like last year's. Already we have found how hard it is to be different: ahead of us we know too well is another year of superficial Christianity.

Eternal God, you know us as we are. You have seen better men and women than we are start the new year with the same sense of frustration and disappointment. Help us, as we are, to put ourselves in your hands, for your hands have been shaping lives from generation to generation. In your unchanging love we would lose our broken promises and failed hopes, for, whatever else may crumble and break this year, your faithfulness lasts forever. So grant that we may live this year believing, trusting, relying only on your love: so that at this year's end we shall be not just one year older, but one year nearer you. Amen.

(A R C M)

8

Offering Prayer at the New Year

Great God, mighty God, yours is the Kingdom, and the power and the glory, yet you show yourself to us in a tiny newborn baby and a homeless one at that.

It is our hope, our prayer and our joyful duty to give back to you our time, our money and ourselves, so that your will may be done in this parish and throughout the world. But Lord, even as we come with this offering, we are so conscious of what we have failed to do...and of those things that we have done that we wish we could now undo ...or the things that we have said that we wish we could now re-phrase, or take back, or forget.

Time after time we have chosen the selfish way and ignored our neighbour: we sidestep the three million people in the unemployment queue and instead join the other queue in the High Street at the twenty-four hour cash dispenser of the Bank or the Building Society.

We join the impatient queue at the check-out in

the supermarket while our brothers and sisters in Christ in Africa and Asia and Latin America wait patiently in line for the result of our concert, or sponsored run, or coffee morning.

Lord, have mercy upon us:
CHRIST HAVE MERCY UPON US:
Lord have mercy upon us.

At this joyful time of the new year, as we still look over our shoulder at Christmas, we thank you that, because of Jesus and his life, death and resurrection, we are forgiven and free people: we are able to leave our fears and failures and burdens behind us and go on. Because of Jesus we recognise with gladness that we are not alone on this earth. You, Lord God, are with us: behind us, beside us and in front of us to show us the way.

We do not carry the weight of the world on *our* shoulders, for with great thankfulness we bring to mind the Lamb of God, who takes away the sin of the world. Amen.

(A M)

9

Prayers for a New Year

Living, loving God, you are a God who takes us into the unknown, out into the dark of the future. But with you beside us at every step we do not need to be afraid of anything, in heaven or on earth.

THY KINGDOM COME O LORD/THY WILL BE DONE

Your coming to be with us at Christmas has saved the world. Your Easter triumph has removed forever our greatest fear, the fear of death; and so we can step out into the new year full of faith and hope and love for all our neighbours.

THY KINGDOM COME O LORD/THY WILL BE DONE

Our greatest wish for 19.... must be for peace in the world. Even in the darkest corners of the world we believe that there is hope and we pray especially for the ordinary people of Northern Ireland, of South Africa, of Afghanistan, of the Middle East and of Central America....

THY KINGDOM COME O LORD/THY WILL BE DONE

We pray that this may truly be a year of peace for the millions of refugees in the world and the hungry millions who cannot eat weapons....

THY KINGDOM COME O LORD/THY WILL BE DONE

Remembering that these are still the days of Christmas we bring to mind the simple image of one little body in a manger and we pray for all the members of Christ's body, the Church, wherever they are and however they worship you; may we all draw closer to Christ this year and so closer to each other. We pray for our congregation here that this next year will be remembered as a time of Christian service to our neighbours and outreach to the local community.

THY KINGDOM COME O LORD/THY WILL BE DONE

We pray today for all the people for whom *last* year was not a good year but was a year of unhappiness and frustration, of dying and mourning; of loneliness and loss; of redundancy and unemployment; of illness and pain...of shattered dreams and broken promises....

THY KINGDOM COME O LORD/THY WILL BE DONE

And finally we pray for those who are housebound or in hospital and joining us in this service today; and we all join now for a moment in the silence of our own hearts as we offer our own prayer for 19....

THY KINGDOM COME O LORD/THY WILL BE DONE.

(A M)

10

Prayers for Corrymeela Sunday

'Religion, as defined by the Revd John Powell S J comes from the Latin "religare"—to bind back, binding back to God with that essential band of love. This binding back is a life-time's work, and it starts where we are' (Fintan McDonald, Corrymeela Link News).

Those who live as their human nature wants them to, have their minds controlled by what human nature wants.

THOSE WHO LIVE AS THE SPIRIT TELLS THEM TO, HAVE THEIR MINDS CONTROLLED BY WHAT THE SPIRIT WANTS.

AND WHAT THE SPIRIT WANTS IS OPPOSED TO WHAT OUR HUMAN NATURE WANTS.

To be controlled by human nature results in death.

TO BE CONTROLLED BY THE SPIRIT BRINGS LIFE AND PEACE.

Lord, we are familiar with our own human nature and tormented by it—

the vanity, the posing and the fear,
the anger and the capacity for violence,
the good we mean to do that fails to get done,
the evil we don't mean that seems somehow to
happen.

WE LOOKED FOR PEACE, BUT NOTHING GOOD HAPPENED;

WE HOPED FOR HEALING, BUT TERROR CAME INSTEAD.

We are familiar with the wisdom of the world and attracted by it; even though it carries the smell of death, we find it hard to resist, because it panders to our natural desires—'put yourself first, never show weakness, know the right people, winner take all, maintain your status, pay back evil for evil'.

WE LOOKED FOR PEACE, BUT NOTHING GOOD HAPPENED;

WE HOPED FOR HEALING, BUT TERROR CAME INSTEAD.

But we are aware, too, of your story,
and caught up in it—
the compassion, the pity and the sacrifice,
the courage and the searching truth,
the complete integrity of word and action,
the commitment to go on loving, whatever the cost.

THE SPIRIT GIVES LIFE:
LET THE SPIRIT DIRECT OUR COURSE.

And we are aware of your style and drawn to it; yet, though we know your words to be the words of life, we are easily distracted, because the self keeps on getting in the way—'The first shall be last, learn humility, have done with the greed that wants more and more, serve joyously, give generously, go on forgiving'.

THE SPIRIT GIVES LIFE:
LET THE SPIRIT DIRECT OUR COURSE.

GIVE US A NEW HEART AND PUT A NEW SPIRIT WITHIN US; TAKE US OUT OF PRE-OCCUPATION WITH OURSELVES AND INTO THE FREEDOM OF YOUR LIFE, FOR YOUR LOVE'S SAKE. AMEN.

Reading: The walls come a-tumbling down
'Let no one be discouraged by the belief that there is nothing one man or one woman can do against the enormous array of the world's ills: against misery, ignorance, injustice and violence. Few will have the greatness to bend history itself, but each of us can work to change a small portion of events, and in the total of all those acts will be written the history of this generation.

It is from the numberless diverse acts of courage and belief that human history is shaped. Each time a man stands up for an ideal, or acts to impose the lot of others, or strikes out against injustice, he sends a tiny ripple of hope, and, crossing each other from a million different centres of energy and daring, these ripples build a current which can sweep down the mightiest walls of oppression and resistance.' (*Robert Kennedy*)

Second Prayer
Lord Jesus Christ,
The names are part of the shame of our history, sign-posts to division, bitterness, violence and hate, symbols of pain, suffering, hostility and despair, crying out to you from earth to heaven—Drogheda and Castlereagh, the Maze Prison and the Shankhill Road, Londonderry and the Boyne.

The slogans are repeated with noisy aggression, as if they carried the conviction of profound truth, denying hope of reconciliation—'No surrender, Brits out, Ireland for the Irish, Loyalist forever'.

Even as we confess our part in the continuing troubles in Ireland and ask for your forgiveness, we bring our concern and our prayers for that divided land:
For those who have been bereaved,
children without fathers, women without husbands,
parents without sons: Lord have mercy,
CHRIST HAVE MERCY.
For those who inherit the crippling prejudices of the past, children brought up to perpetuate 'orange' and 'green', 'them' and 'us': Lord have mercy,
CHRIST HAVE MERCY.
For those entrusted with maintaining law and order, policemen and soldiers working in an atmosphere of betrayal and mistrust: Lord have mercy,
CHRIST HAVE MERCY.

For those in hospital and prison, perpetrators of violence and victims of fear and the providers of weapons: Lord have mercy,
CHRIST HAVE MERCY.
For those who accept political leadership, strive for a better future, work for good and pray for peace: Lord have mercy,
CHRIST HAVE MERCY.
OUR FATHER....

(R F B)

11

Amnesty

Prayer for Prisoner of Conscience Week:
Jesus of Nazareth, you came into the human situation and you showed us the heart of God. You speak to that situation as you give us faith. We trust you because you have shown yourself in weakness and powerlessness; you have shown yourself in your passion, in the suffering of your last days on earth; in your agony in torture upon the Cross; in your fulfilment of your purpose in your dying....

Jesus, our God, we humbly present you on the Cross to the world that observes Prisoner of Conscience Week. By living in his weakness we have confidence and he will not mock their condition.

Lord we remember those who suffer for their beliefs; who are denied freedom; whose bodies and spirits are violated.

Remember all such people of goodwill whose integrity is so impeached; whose rights are so violated and whose being is so assaulted.

Remember, too, people of ill will.

We bring to you not only the suffering of the innocent, but also the plight of the tormentors caught in a web of evil. When they come to your judgement, let the fruits of the loyalty and heroism of the tormented and innocent captives be part of their pain towards forgiveness.

In silence we remember before you the prisoners for whom we have interceded in your grace to their captors. Earnestly we pray for the work of Amnesty and all who follow out their discipleship through it to you. Grant them the necessary loving patience, the continuing compassion, and equanimity in the midst of horror.

Be over all places and people where ordinary decency is violated and stand with all your children towards the coming of your Kingdom, through Jesus Christ our Lord. Amen.

(K C)

12

Meditation on Remembrance

For use prior to the two-minute silence on Remembrance Sunday.

In a few moments we shall pause for a time of
Remembrance, a silence,
to be used by us all on this day to help us remember.
But how?
What are we to think about when we are still?
How are we to order our thoughts in the silence?

What are we to remember when we are called upon so
to do?
For all of us today, with these questions in mind, these
words of
Lawrence Binyon can perhaps assist us to direct our
thoughts.

'They shall not grow old
as we that are left grow old.
Age shall not weary them
nor the years condemn.
At the going down of the sun
and in the morning
we will remember them.'

'They shall not grow old
as we that are left grow old...'
We are left—
following those who have gone before
who are present with us here no longer;
growing old with the passing years
as they no longer do.
As current events pass into history,
as today becomes yesterday
and tomorrow overtakes today,
we are left—
while those who were once young
are now become old names
of old times,
of old wars,
and those who were old before their time
are now become
the ancients of history books
or jerky figures in black and white films
or stark inscriptions on war memorials.

'Age shall not weary them
nor the years condemn...'
They are at peace—
while we grow weary with the pressures of living
and preserving our peace;
while we grow weary with remembrance
and the recalling of past horrors;
while we grow weary
with the hurt that is still caused,
and the memories that are still hard,
and the lessons that are still unlearned,
and the weariness that is still overwhelming;
while we grow weary of condemnation—
of those of the past for what they had to do,
and of those who would still wish to remember;
while we grow weary with the responsibilities we carry
            on our shoulders
that were once carried on the frail shoulders
of a past generation.

'At the going down of the sun
and in the morning...'
As the sun sets only to rise again—
as day follows night;
as a night of pain
gives way to a morning of promise;
as a night of horror
gives way to a morning of hope;
as a night of weariness
gives way to a morning of refreshment
and new beginnings;
as a night of sinfulness
gives way to a morning of repentance
and reconciliation....

'We will remember them...'
We will remember them—

the names;
the faces;
the stories;
the events;
we will remember them...
for we dare not do any other.
For lest this humanity forgets—
as this fragile world becomes ever older;
as we that are left grow older with it;
as we grow weary of condemnation
and seek the new beginning
of reconciliation and peace;
as we affirm in this place
that the morning of promise
will come ever again from the dark night of pain;
lest this world forgets,
we will remember....

'They shall not grow old
as we that are left grow old.
Age shall not weary them
nor the years condemn.
At the going down of the sun
and in the morning
we will remember them.'
For our own reasons,
in our own way,
and now with our own thoughts,
let us stand
and in silence
let us remember.

(T G)

13

Remembrance

*Many Scottish War Memorials stand in open places,
overlooking the sea, or surrounded by hills—or all three. This
Act of Remembrance was used in such a situation.*

Call to Prayer
'I will lift up mine eyes unto the hills.'
    We remember those who lie amongst green hills,
which are not for them the hills of home.
    We pray for those 'that go down to the sea in
ships, that do business in great waters' and we
remember those who rest in the deep until the sea
gives up the dead.
    'The heavens declare the glory of God.'
    We remember those who left the familiarity of
earth to fight and die in the loneliness of air.

Prayer
Almighty God, maker of earth and sky and sea, we
give thanks for the freedom in which we enjoy your
creation; and we remember in gratitude and humility
those who paid that freedom's price. May this wreath
be a sign not only of our memories but also of our own
commitment to further the cause of justice, freedom
and peace in our community and our world. In Jesus'
name and for his sake we ask it. Amen.

(A W)

14

Remembrance

Call to Prayer

Our help is in the name of the Lord, who made heaven and earth. Jesus said: 'There is no greater love than this, that a man should lay down his life for his friends. You are my friends, if you do what I command you. Love one another.'

Prayer of Adoration, Confession and Petition

Incomparable God, Father of each one of us, we praise and adore you. Your love is unending, your mercy limitless, your power infinite, your grace unbounded. You alone give life its full and true direction; you alone bring good out of evil, life out of death and hope out of despair. We are amazed that you continue to concern yourself with us, despite our deep and constant unworthiness of you. Faithful, gracious Father, we offer you our praise and adoration with reverent, humble and thankful hearts; in the name of Jesus Christ our Lord.

Let us confess our sins to God:

Father, our own human history condemns us, making plain our sinfulness. We're unable to live together in harmony; our self-assertion, greed, ignorance and prejudice ensure that peace is always short-lived. We let pride and patriotism blind and deafen us while justice and mercy go unheeded. We abuse your gift of knowledge; we don't use our technology for good, so often choosing destructive and inhumane courses instead.

Lord, have mercy upon us:

CHRIST, HAVE MERCY UPON US: LORD, HAVE MERCY UPON US.

God the Father, God the Son and God the Holy

Spirit have mercy upon you, pardon and deliver you from all your sins and give you time to amend your lives, through Jesus Christ our Lord.

Almighty Father, you call your children to live as brothers and sisters, in love and harmony, and have given your Son to be our Saviour, the Prince of Peace: grant that we, who are called by his name, may yield our lives to your service and strive for reconciliation, understanding and peace in all our relationships, through Jesus Christ our Lord. Amen.

Prayers of Intercession
Lord Jesus Christ, you said: 'How blest are the peacemakers; God shall call them his sons.' Today we pray for all who seek to bring peace between nations and peace between individuals.
Lord hear us.
LORD, GRACIOUSLY HEAR US.
We pray for the Secretary General and the staff of the United Nations Organisation, and for those who are prepared to work long hours of travel to any country—all for the cause of peace.
Lord, hear us.
LORD, GRACIOUSLY HEAR US.
We pray for governments who are prepared to send units for the difficult role of a peace-keeping force:
Lord, hear us.
LORD GRACIOUSLY HEAR US.
We pray for Christians and non-Christians, who quietly and steadfastly advocate and live in the way of peace and thereby work for its growth:
Lord, hear us.
LORD GRACIOUSLY HEAR US.
We pray for those who are willing to risk their lives in the trouble-spots of the world in order to build

bridges of understanding between people of different races and colour:
   Lord, hear us.
   LORD GRACIOUSLY HEAR US.
We pray for people like ourselves who, having known the bitterness which hatred and strife can create in families and between individuals, seek in your strength to sow seeds of peace:
   Lord, hear us.
   LORD GRACIOUSLY HEAR US.
Count us, Lord God, among those who are peacemakers, that we may be worthy childen of one family. These our prayers we offer in the name of the Prince of Peace, Jesus Christ our Lord. Amen.

Prayers of Thanksgiving
Father, it is right to give you thanks and praise for the world you have created and given into our care. We thank you for the survival of the earth and the continued existence of humanity on it.
   We give you thanks that, despite our cruelty and violence as a race, we know also the power of mercy and compassion; in the face of hatred and lies, we know something of love and truth; in the midst of death and war, we recognise peace and life as attractive. Gracious God, giver and revealer of all good, we thank and praise you. We give thanks for Jesus Christ, the Lord of life, the conqueror of death, the giver of eternal life and peace and hope. We give thanks for the Holy Spirit, for his ceaseless revelation of Christ's powerful gospel, in the world, in the Church, and in us. We give thanks for all people who, by their lives and deaths, bear witness to a hatred of war and a true love of peace. Therefore with angels and archangels and with all the company of heaven we proclaim your greatness and sing your praises, saying:
Our Father....

God grant to the living, grace, to the departed, rest, to the Church, the Queen, the Commonwealth and mankind, his love and protection. And the blessing of God Almighty, the Father, the Son and the Holy Spirit....

(T G L)

15

Prayers for Remembrance Sunday

Call to Prayer
The Lord's eyes are turned towards those who fear him, towards those who hope for his unfailing love.

Prayer
O God the all-merciful, whose eyes are all tenderness, turn your eyes upon us as we come to worship you. Your eyes, which are all tenderness, have looked on Goliath and Genghis Khan, on the mud of Flanders and the heat of the Burma Road. Turn these loving, hurting eyes to us that our worship may be made by you into a Christian act of remembrance, done in the spirit of Christ and his gospel.

You have looked on the horrors of war, but you have looked on worse. For you have seen into the hearts of each of us here today, and there you have seen a naked rebellion and disobedience without the self-sacrifice or courage which can be found on the battlefield. We confess the ungodliness of our hearts and lives. We confess our sin, which is at the centre of the world's hurt. Forgive us for the sake of him who took the world's hurt upon his own body, Jesus Christ our Lord.

On this Remembrance Day we come, O Lord, in gratitude for all who have died that we might live, for all who endured pain that we might know joy, for all who suffered imprisonment that we might know freedom. Turn our deep feeling now into determination and our determination into deed, that as men died for peace, we may live for peace for the sake of the Prince of Peace, even Jesus Christ our Lord. Amen.

'I am the resurrection and the life: he that believeth in me though he were dead yet shall he live: whosoever liveth and believeth in me shall never die.'

'They shall grow not old as we that are left grow old. Age shall not weary them nor the years condemn. At the going down of the sun and in the morning we shall remember them.'

Jesus said: 'Others toiled and you have come in for the harvest of their toil'.

O God, whose Father's eyes have looked on the unmarked grave of your only Son, help us to believe that from that unmarked grave there comes the hope of the world. His was a lonely death and a bloody death: at his death too there were soldiers doing their job who never knew his name. But from that grave there rises one who claims all the world's dead young men as his own, and girls, and the old. From that unmarked grave there rises one who brings healing of broken hearts and hope for us all. O God we give you thanks for the life and death and rising again of Jesus Christ, your Son, our Lord.

He was the Saviour of the world but still he was Mary's child. In her and in her grief are all the world's mothers: mothers whose memories are of two world wars and of battles and bombs and bullets in many other places and many other times. In her are all the world's mourners: mourners of all the war dead and of their own precious ones lost to life in countless other ways. Speak to them this day the words of Jesus as your word, 'Blessed are they that mourn; for they shall be comforted'.

He was the Saviour of the world but still he was Peter's friend. In Peter are all the friends of Jesus since, for we betray our friend and the Church is faithless, loveless and nearly hopeless. By the broken body of Jesus, O Lord, and by his risen power unmake our unchristian Church and renew us in your spirit. He is the Saviour of the world so we pray for all who need a saviour; for the lost and the wandering; for the sick and needy; for our own dear ones. O Saviour of the world, grant that they may be led on to the road home to you.

He is the Saviour of the world so our lives belong to him, with the lives of our dear ones whom we no longer see. Grant that when the day of God shall break and the shadows flee away we shall meet with them and all your redeemed in your presence, where there is fullness of joy; through Jesus Christ our Lord, in whose words we say: *Our Father.... Amen.*

God grant to the living, grace, to the departed, rest, to the Church, the Queen, the Commonwealth and all mankind his love and protection; and the blessing of God Almighty, the Father, the Son and the Holy Spirit be with you and abide with you always. Amen.

(A R C M)

16

Prayer for an End of Term Assembly

*(The asterisk * denotes clapping of hands four times)*

We praise you, God * sun, moon and stars * they praise you too * for they were made * all things were made * were made by you * the snow, the rain * the sting of frost * and summer days * and autumn fruit * we praise you, God * for holidays * this day of days * our spirits sing * and fingers tell * our song of praise * for work and play * for highs and lows * we need them all * to make us grow * to make us reach * for better joys * for deeper far * than facts can show * are things we know * ourselves alone * we thank you, God * for growing sure * and surer still * of things that count * to trust a friend * a friend like you * from start to end * to love the world * that you have made * through thick and thin * through light and shade * we thank you God * for being king * the king of kings * the one supreme * who sets us free * to dream our dream * no other dream * can do as well * and so we say * this is a day * for you to bless * to set our feet * on surer ground * for we were lost * and now are found * amazing grace! * amazing God! * receive our praise * and bless the days * the days to come * you will be there * to guard and guide * the steps we take * the moves we make * we thank you, God * receive our praise * for Jesus' sake! Amen.

(D O)

(iii)   **Prayers for Peace, Justice and Healing**

17

A Prayer for Peace

O God, listen to your people as we pray for peace—
peace between nations, peace within communities and
families, peace in our hearts. Heal us of the divisions
that damage and hurt us and lift from us the burden
of our guilt, that we may no longer be cast down in the
blackness of despair but lifted by your mercy into the
clear light of your love.

O God, our pain is also your pain and you must
weep to see the hurt we inflict upon ourselves and
upon others. Have pity on us now as in silence we cast
upon you all our anger, all our violence, all our
remorse, and carry them away in the current of your
overflowing love.

Now O God, listen to your people as we pray for
peace in the lives of these our brothers and sisters who
need our prayer and your love. They cry to you for
shalom and a renewal of life and peace. We add our
cries to theirs for a lightening of their burdens....

*There follow specific intercessions for situations in which
people suffer through violence and war.*

O Lord, hear us we pray....O Lord, give us your
peace.

We ask these prayers in the confidence of your
love, through Jesus Christ our Lord. Amen.

(K G and I G)

18

Prayers for Peace and Justice

The following set of brief devotions comes from worship in Iona Abbey. They could also be used in regular or occasional house-church, or Peace and Justice Group, or Youth Group meetings.

Opening

Leader:	We believe, O God, that you are the eternal God of life
All:	WE BELIEVE, O GOD, THAT YOU ARE THE ETERNAL GOD OF LOVE
Leader:	We believe, O God of all the peoples
All:	YOU HAVE CREATED US FROM DUST AND ASHES
Leader:	O God, who brought us to the joyous light of this day
All:	BRING US TO THE GUIDING LIGHT OF ETERNITY

MONDAY: Those who witness for peace and justice.
Reading: James 2:15–17
Hymn
Prayer: Let us remember and pray for those who have been exiled from their native land, who have been forced to leave behind their heritage and possessions, their families and their friends, and who have had to begin life anew in a foreign culture and among strangers;

those who are discriminated against on the grounds of their race, sex, religion, political opinions;

those who at this very moment are being tortured in body, mind or spirit because of convictions they hold dear, those who languish in dark prisons so that we may walk free in the sun, those whose bodies have been broken so that we may walk in fear of no hand;

for repressive authorities, jailers and torturers, bound in a far deeper prison.

Let us give thanks for all who speak out on behalf of the voiceless and powerless, and especially for the work of Amnesty International. May we too play our part in seeking justice and mercy and freedom for all.

We ask these and all our prayers in the name of Jesus Christ our Lord. Amen.

Collect for Monday: Peace between neighbours
Peace between kindred
Peace between lovers
In love of the God of life.

TUESDAY: Those who work for healing within families and communities, between nations, of the environment.
Reading: Luke 4:16–21
Hymn
Prayer: Christ the Healer,
We come to you to pray for those who work for
        healing:
We pray for all who build bridges—
    across the gulfs of fear and despair,
    across the barriers of race and culture,
    across the pain of hunger and powerlessness.
    Thank you God for their building.
We pray for all who work on the land—
    for those who struggle to produce crops,
    for those who plan to make the physical environ-
        ment a better place for people to live in,
    for farmers, for environmentalists, for architects,
        gardeners and town planners.
    Be now their vision, God.
We pray for the world's carers and listeners—
    for those who bring healing into the brokenness of
        people's lives.

Sustain them, God, with your strong love.

We pray for those who are angry—angry at the injustice they experience around them; angry about what is happening in their lives. May their anger bring them closer to you, Jesus; may it result in healing rather than frustration.

We pray for any known to us who today are in need of healing. We bring them to you in the silence....

Lastly, we pray for ourselves—that your touch may heal us and free us to experience your love.

We ask it, that your kingdom may come—in us and through us. Amen.

Collect for Tuesday: O my soul's healer, keep me at
                              evening,
                              Keep me at morning, keep me at
                              noon,
                              I am tired, astray and stumbling,
                              Shield me from sin.

WEDNESDAY: Those who work for a more just economic order, workers and management, the unemployed, those whose labour is exploited.

Reading: Matthew 20:1–15

Hymn

Prayer: O God, we thank you that you have given to us, through Jesus Christ our Lord, the gospel of your grace to all humankind.

You showed us what generosity is like, to make no difference between people of the first hour and the folk of the last hour, to pay the last ones as much as the first ones.

Lord, your gospel makes evident how our economic order is failing, not only concerning the first world and the so-called third world, not only concerning the north and south, the east and the west, but also within our highly developed industrial countries.

So we pray today for all people working in industry—
for the workers, that they may be paid fairly;
for the management, that they may not fail, in
managing, in keeping jobs open, in
considering the problems of environment and
ecology;
for all those who are unemployed—
because their firm could not keep up the struggle
of competition,
because economic structures have changed,
because they never had the chance to get training,
or to get a job,
For all those whose labour is exploited—
black workers in South Africa
women in Thailand who have to prostitute their
bodies for sex tourists from the West;
women in our country with part-time jobs, without
employment insurance and pension rights;
the families whose life and love and joy is
threatened by shift work.
In silence, we pray for those people working in
industry, whom we know personally....
Collect for Wednesday: Bless to us, O God, the earth
beneath our feet.
Bless to us, O God, the path
whereon we go.
Bless to us, O God, the thing of
our desire.
Evermore and evermore, bless
to us our rest.

*THURSDAY: Those who are engaged in public service—
local and national politicians, the United Nations, those
involved in processes of law, all who care for others in the
home.*
Reading: John 13:1–17
Hymn

Prayer: God, we give you thanks for the people who quietly serve those around them, who without fuss, see what is needed and do it.

God, we know people like this, and in the silence now we remember them before you.

God, bless them and keep them in your love.

We pray too for those engaged in public service, for local and national politicians and local councils.

We pray too for judges, and all who are involved in the processes of law:

We pray for justice in our land—justice for all people.

We pray too for the work of the United Nations Organisation, and its Secretary General.

And we pray for ourselves; God, help us to love you, help us to serve you in our neighbours, help us to be your people.

We ask it in the name of Jesus. Amen.

Collect for Thursday: My Christ, my shield, my encircler,
Each day, each night, each light, each dark,
Be near me, uphold me, my treasure, my triumph.

FRIDAY: Those who help us to celebrate—artists, musicians, writers, children, friends—the unity of the Church.
Reading: Mark 10:13–16
Hymn
Prayer: God, you are the one who loves us and calls us to live life to the full. We thank you today for people who help us to celebrate life, for those who help us to discover ourselves and to recognise your presence in all around us.

We thank you for writers and musicians, for clowns and storytellers, who share their vision of life with the world and enrich our lives with humour and mystery and beauty.

We thank you for children, God, children whose insistent questions and infectious laughter prevent us from taking ourselves too seriously. We thank you for the warmth of children's love, for their readiness to trust us with their secrets and fears. Help us not to betray that trust, and show us ways to make the world a better place for children everywhere to grow up in.

God, help us to celebrate life gladly in all its mystery and all its glory—that your kingdom may come in and through us.

We ask it in the name of Jesus. Amen.

Collect for Friday: God to enfold us, God to surround us,

God in our speaking, God in our thinking,

God in our life, God in our lips,

God in our souls, God in our hearts.

SATURDAY: Prophets and pioneers—migrant workers, refugees, travellers, our own inward journey.

Reading: Isaiah 58:1–11

Hymn

Prayer: Creator God, we thank you for the prophets you have sent through all the ages to guide us, to challenge us, to tell, again and again, of your great love for all people.

Forgive us because we rarely listen to what they say. We become comfortable and do not want to hear about oppression, hunger, violence or injustice.

We are afraid, and do not want to face the consequences of doing your will. We do not trust you, God. Too often we are happier with what we have now, to be willing to work for the kingdom you promise.

Help us to listen to the words of your prophets, like the words of Isaiah, spoken and written through many centuries—words which still call us to you, with your demand that we live justly and your promise that you are with us when we try. Thank you that Isaiah's deep concern for the small and the weak and the oppressed still moves and touches and enables us today.

God of life and love, help us always to listen for your word of challenge and love, wherever it is spoken, and to respond in our own lives by working for true justice and mercy, in hope and love.

We ask this in the name of Jesus Christ. Amen.

Collect for Saturday: As you were before us at our life's beginning,
Be you so again at our journey's end.
As you were beside us at our soul's shaping,
God be also at our journey's close.

Closing

Glory to God the Creator, who gives us life.
Glory to Jesus the Christ who calls us.
Glory to the Spirit, the comforter, who empowers us.
As it was in the beginning, is now and shall be forever. Amen.

(K G and I G)

19

Prayers for Healing

O Lord, our life, our love, our liberty, free us from our chains of despair.

Lift us out of our self-obsession to know the

freedom of the given life.

Release us from our fears of meaninglessness and failure, so that we may know conflict and not be torn apart by it,

so that we may face injustice and not be compromised by it,

so that we may confront violence and not be seduced by it.

Free all who suffer, in body, mind or spirit, and make whole and holy their brokenness.

We pray for healing between nations,

for healing within communities,

for healing between persons,

and for the courage to face the demands of reconciliation in our own lives.

In particular, we pray for these our sisters and brothers....

(Here follow names of those who are sick or in distress)

O my soul's healer, keep me at evening,
Keep me at morning, keep me at noon.
I am tired, astray and stumbling,
Shield me from sin.

Loving Christ, who was hanged upon the tree, each day and night we remember your covenant. In life and in death you are our health and our peace, each day may we remember the source of the gifts you have given gently and generously.

Our God, we come to you now seeking healing in our lives.

There is sadness in our lives because we are weak and do not do the good that we want to; because we cannot hold on to the beauty that we see; because we are mortal and must watch our dying.

Lord, have mercy upon us...Christ have mercy upon us.

There is anger in our lives because we are hurt by the rejection of others, because we live by injustice, because we cannot have our own way.

Lord, have mercy upon us...Christ have mercy upon us.

There is pride in our lives because we want to cover our failures, because we want to hide our fears, because we want to be in control. Lord, have mercy upon us...Christ have mercy upon us.

There is unkindness in our lives because we seek for a power that escapes us, because we are scared to be touched, because we do not know how to love.

Lord, have mercy upon us...Christ have mercy upon us.

There is in our lives what you know, and what we in our hearts know.

Silence

Lord, have mercy upon us....Christ have mercy upon us.

In the name of Jesus Christ, I tell you, get up and walk, your sins are forgiven.

Listen now to our prayer for healing for others. Mend our broken world, our broken communities, our broken lives with your love, and bring wholeness to the place of division.

By your mercy, which is solidarity and compassion, root out the injustices which cause division;

by your truth, may we grow in understanding and generosity to seek true peace with justice;

by your love, move all people to gentleness in place of hatred, and hope in place of fear.

And we pray now for these, real people, suffering people, for whom prayer has been asked....

(*Here follow names*)

And, as the mist scatters on the crest of the hills, may each ill haze clear from our souls, O God, our light and our glory. Amen.

(K G and I G)

20

The Drum Sermon

(*For use at a Peace Service, with accompanying instrumentation*)

Sunday after Sunday, we pray for peace in the world.
We all want peace.
We all agree with the eleven-year-old who prayed— 'Lord, make this world to last as long as possible'.
We would all want to say that. Many of us probably include that hope in the prayers we say at home, privately, secretly.
The world doesn't hear that kind of language.
The world hears people quarrelling.
DRUM: (*broken sounds, crashes*)
The world hears people fighting. In Northern Ireland the rattle of dustbin lids is the signal that a police search or an army swoop is about to happen.
DRUM: (*rapid beats*)
We hear people suffering all across the world. We hear of prisoners of conscience. We hear of political arrests and detentions. We hear the cell doors banging shut.
DRUM:—*boom*
Black people
DRUM—*boom*
White people

DRUM:—*boom*
Yellow people
DRUM:—*boom*
Sound has no colour.

Many fine things are said about peace. Many high hopes are voiced. All too often people speak of peace with their lips but in their hearts there is no love. They are like noisy gongs:

DRUM: (*hollow ringing*)
or like clanging cymbals:
DRUM: (*discordant noises*)

We try to talk to each other. All too often this conversation becomes a contest of shouts and whispers.

DRUM: (*bass . . . drowning kettle-drum*)

The sound that swamps all other sounds is the sound of feet marching to battle.

DRUM: (*martial beat, rising to crescendo*)

Since 1945 there have been dozens of wars. Dozens of dozens, almost one hundred and forty wars. Fifteen million dead. Over Europe, the Middle East, the Far East, the pale horse has ridden. Its rider is called Death.

DRUM: (*hooves*)

He has ridden to the gates of our cities, to the borders of our land, to the entrance of our minds, to the door-posts of our memory.

In a city called Hiroshima his hoofbeats sounded at a quarter to eight on the morning of the sixth of August, 1945.

The clocks in the city stopped at that moment.
Imagine the sound of a clock stopping.

DRUM: (*single beats for a moment, then silence*)
Silence.

Somebody said once: in order for wrong to triumph it is only necessary for good people to do and say nothing.

We must begin by saying something.

We must send messages.

Do you know the International Distress Call for ships at sea?

DRUM: (*S O S*)

Maybe that is something we can say to other peoples—save our souls! Save our world! Save us and we will save you!

We *can* send messages of friendship.

We can listen to the messages of others.

Maybe we'll discover that other people want the world to last as long as possible too.

Maybe we'll discover that they are saying something we need to hear.

Maybe we'll discover that we have a lot to celebrate: a lot of common hopes and joys.

DRUM: (*up-tempo jazz beat*)

And, in silence, maybe we'll be able to hear a very secret sound, a very important, urgent sound—the heart-beat of the children who are waiting to be born, waiting to inherit the world. The heart-beat of the baby.

DRUM: (*rapidly, indicating foetal heart-beat*)

(D O)

(iv)   **Prayers for Informal, Small Group and Family Worship**

21

Prayers for a Family Service

Call to Prayer
The Lord is good. His love is eternal and his faithfulness lasts for ever.

Prayer

Gracious God, our Father, we are glad to come to this place today, a house strongly built, a place of beauty, a setting of quietness and of peace.

Help us here to sense and to seek your strength and your beauty and your peace, that you declared and demonstrated in Jesus and which you are offering to us now.

We have come from many places, by different experiences, men and women, boys and girls, fathers and mothers, sisters and brothers, friends and acquaintances, in company or alone—all needing one another, all belonging together but unable to realise it, till humbly, each one and all together, we call you Our Father.

> In your house we remember how good you have been to us
> —for a wonderful world,
> —for all we can think and do and dream of achieving,
> —for the joy of giving and receiving in our homes and with our friends,
> —for Jesus, our daily example and constant friend, to protect us from evil and establish us in all goodness.

All together, we come to say Father, thank you.

Too often, we forget the family to which we belong, and so grow selfish, fail to speak the truth with one another, lack love and pity and helpfulness

> All together, we come to say Father, forgive us.

Some of us have learned a great deal about the world, about people, about ourselves. Some of us are just beginning to learn. All of us need to learn more, more about your patience and goodness, more about our own weaknesses, more about the needs of others.

> All together, we come to say Father, teach us.

None of us can see into the future, even as far as

tomorrow; none of us can stand alone, so in hope and confidence, in the joy of your presence, we all together turn to you and say, Father, lead us and help us.

In Jesus' name we ask these things and in his words, as one family we pray: *Our Father....*

(A B D)

22

An Act of Worship for House Groups

Opening
Give thanks to the Lord for he is good
    HIS LOVE IS EVERLASTING.
    Come, let us praise God joyfully
    LET US COME TO HIM WITH THANKSGIVING.
    For the good world and things great and small in it
    THANK YOU GOD.
    For the Church into which we have been called; and our life together in the Lord
    THANK YOU GOD.
    Above all for your son Jesus Christ who lived and died and lives again for us; for our hope in him and for the joy of serving him
    WE THANK AND PRAISE YOU GOD OUR FATHER FOR ALL YOUR GOODNESS TO US.
    Give thanks to the Lord for he is good.
    HIS LOVE IS EVERLASTING.
    O God, from whom to be turned is to fall, to whom to be turned is to rise, and in whom to stand is to abide forever, grant us in all our duties your help, in all our perplexities your guidance, in all our dangers your protection, and in all our sorrows your peace; through Jesus Christ our Lord.
    AMEN.

Reading: First meeting, Psalm 103:1–14; second, Psalm 104:1–9; third, Psalm 107:1–9

Let us pray:

Be with us now, Eternal God, as we meet as your Church in this home. Help us so to listen to you that we may know you and love you; and help us so to listen to each other that we may know and love our neighbours. For Jesus' sake.

AMEN.

Closing

Let us pray:

Let us bring to God this evening which we have shared: the people, the discoveries, the friendship, the faith.

Silence

Your kingdom come, O Lord

YOUR WILL BE DONE.

Let us bring to God his Church; his Church throughout the world and our own congregation.

Silence

Your kingdom come, O Lord

YOUR WILL BE DONE.

Let us bring to God his world; and all the sick, poor and frightened folk in it.

Silence

Your kingdom come, O Lord

YOUR WILL BE DONE.

Let us bring to God our families, here or far away.

Silence

Your kingdom come, O Lord

YOUR WILL BE DONE.

Let us bring to God ourselves: our sins, our fears, our hopes, our dreams.

Silence

Your kingdom come, O Lord

YOUR WILL BE DONE.

OUR FATHER, WHO ART IN HEAVEN...

AMEN

Reading: First meeting John 1:1–14; second, John 1:29–34; third, John 1:43–51
Let us pray: (To be said quite slowly)
LORD, MAKE ME AN INSTRUMENT OF YOUR PEACE...
...AND IT IS IN DYING THAT WE ARE BORN TO ETERNAL LIFE.
THE GRACE OF THE LORD JESUS CHRIST, THE LOVE OF GOD AND THE COMPANY OF THE HOLY SPIRIT BE WITH US ALL. AMEN.

(A R C M)

23

Informal Service of Praise and Personal Ministry

Prayer
'The Lord reigns, let the earth be glad.' Gracious God, we gather together as your people, bound to you through your love in Jesus Christ, bound to one another through our common devotion to him. We come to you in a spirit of praise, that, as we exalt your name in humble thanksgiving, so we may be lifted up into the wonder of your heavenly glory.

We look upon Jesus in love and adoration, that we would truly worship you in spirit through him. We come because we have heard your invitation and we are so sure that you are in the midst of us. We come to please you and to know the joy of your blessing upon us. Through Jesus Christ our Lord. Amen.

Here may follow a reading from Christian literature on a theme appropriate to the service.
Praise:
Children's Highlight Time

Jesus said: 'Let the children come to me...do not stop them'. Come now children from your seats and join us here at the front.

Children sit together on carpet

Praise:

Talk on theme of the service.

Prayer (said together):

OUR FATHER, WE THANK YOU THAT YOU LOVE US ALL—

THAT YOU LOVE ME AND THAT YOU WANT WHAT IS BEST FOR ME.

THANK YOU FOR SHOWING ME THIS IN JESUS,

WHO CAME TO LIVE LIKE ME,

AND WHO GREW UP TO LOVE AND DIE FOR ME AND THE WHOLE WORLD.

THANK YOU THAT HE IS ALIVE TO FORGIVE AND HEAL.

COME CLOSE TO US NOW WHATEVER OUR NEED,

AND BECAUSE YOU LOVE US, PLEASE FORGIVE AND HEAL US.

THANK YOU SO VERY MUCH. AMEN.

Praise:

Prayer:

Lord our God we rejoice in your presence. You are our King and that gladdens our hearts. You have created us and, because you love us, you want to guide us and lead us into the path that pleases you and brings mercy and hope to our neighbour.

We live in a disordered world and we are part of that disorder. Indeed, too often, we can be the cause of it. Make us clean and forgive us through the death of Jesus and so help us to become channels of order and peace, of comfort and strength. Enable us to see and understand that the end of human endeavour and strength is the beginning of divine wisdom and power. You have so gently drawn us into your body. May we and all your members be broken for the healing of the nations, that your Kingdom may be established.

Heavenly Father, before you our hearts are laid bare and in this place we believe you want to touch us in blessing. Show us our needs by the probing power of your Holy Spirit as starkly as you see them and cause us to seek your touch; that reconciled, restored and renewed we would give eloquent testimony that we are the people of God, followers of the Saviour Jesus, living residences of the Holy Spirit.

Lord of all mercy and compassion, we serve in a wounded, hurting world. As we pray for those around us and to the farthest shores of this, your world, we ask that you would bind up those who are wounded and soothe those who are hurting. We do so conscious that you call us to be ministers of your healing power. Make us both obedient and gentle servants of your love that by our good works others would give glory to you, our Father in heaven. Through Jesus Christ our Lord. Amen.

Praise:

Prayer

Come, Holy Spirit of God, and inspire our thoughts and words so that we may hear the voice of our Father and thus be changed more and more into the likeness of Jesus. Amen.

Sermon on the theme of the service

Praise:

Opportunity for ministry to personal needs

Reading from an appropriate piece of literature

Come, that we may do what the Lord commands. That is, that we may pray with you and seek that precious blessing of Jesus in your life as you give thanks, as you ask to be forgiven, as you seek to be healed. We affirm that God calls his body to be an agent of his ministry in this way.

There is now a time when individuals or couples or

*friends can come forward to the front to be prayed with by
today's ministry team.*

This time can be drawn to a close with this prayer:

We praise you, Lord Jesus, that no cry goes
unheard, that no prayer goes unanswered, and as we
have in this hour sought your touch upon our lives, so
we are convinced that you have not left us untouched.
Your love is stronger than death and it is by that love
that we have been blessed here. Our hearts are full of
praise. This place is filled with the joy of that praise.
'The Lord reigns, let the earth be glad.' Amen.

Praise:

Benediction: These moments have been alive with
the presence and power of the Lord. It is now our
privilege to be fruitful that, in us and through us,
others would know that same presence and power.

Go in peace and may the blessing of God, the
Father, the Son and the Holy Spirit be with you.
Amen.

(N M)

24

A Litany for a Home Communion

Lord, you met with your friends in a room of a family
home and there you shared a fellowship meal with
them. You promised them that when two or three of
them were gathered together in the future in your
name, you would still be with them. So we gather
together in this family home, two, or three or more.
We come, trusting in your promise. Help us to know
that when we meet with each other here, so we meet
also with you.

When we share fellowship and love with each other
MAY OUR BONDS OF LOVE WITH YOU ALSO BE STRENGTHENED.

When we separate and are apart from one another
MAY WE NOT FORGET EACH OTHER AND THE SHARING WE HAVE HAD, BUT REMEMBER THAT WE REMAIN ONE PEOPLE UNDER YOUR LOVE.

When things are unchanging and life is good
MAY WE REJOICE IN THE LORD AND FIND STRENGTH IN YOUR UNCHANGING PROMISES.

When we are in the midst of change and life is puzzling and uncertain
MAY WE TAKE TIME TO PRAY AND TRUST IN YOUR EVERLASTING PRESENCE.

As we break bread and pour out the wine of this communion sacrament
MAY WE REMEMBER JESUS CHRIST WHO COMES TO US AGAIN, RISEN AND PRESENT, IN THIS HOME.

As we share with each other the body and blood of our Lord
MAY WE REMEMBER HIS PROMISE TO BE WITH US TO THE END OF TIME.

And as we depart from this home, when this time of communion is over, may we find peace and blessing for all that is yet to come, till, by the grace of God, we meet together again. Through Jesus Christ our Lord. Amen.

(T G)

25

A Silver Wedding Anniversary Prayer

Lord God, the Creator who makes all things new, we are glad today and always that you are continually at work within us, continually creating, continually correcting, continually leading us forward into new depths and fresh heights.

For the challenges we meet—and for the will to meet them, we give you thanks.

For the knowledge we gain, and for the insight that helps us to benefit from that knowledge, we give you thanks.

For the certainties we cannot live without, and for the joy of sharing these certainties, we give you thanks.

For this day, when memory and anticipation join hands, we give you thanks.

Today, with A and B we give thanks for a journey shared, and territory made familiar, and truths that have been recognised and made their own; and today also we join with them in asking once more for the faith and courage that we need for the road not travelled yet, the experiences that lie in wait for us.

O God, as you have blessed that past, so now, we pray, guide future days, guard future joys and let each glad or stern occasion be equally, in your providing mercy, an opportunity for love to deepen and find its definition.

Grant, God and Father, that A and B may have confidence in each other, and confidence in their marriage, and many days to claim the privilege of belonging to each other, through Jesus Christ our Lord.

(D O)

26

(a) **Prayer at Start of Meeting**

O Lord our God, as we begin our work together at the start of another year, we look to you for help: to be true to those who have laboured before us and in our midst by working willingly and cheerfully and well; to seek to make this a place where truth with compassion and wisdom with service may abundantly dwell; and show us, O Lord, the peace we should seek, the peace we must give, the peace we must forego, the peace you have given us in Jesus Christ our Lord. Amen.

(D W D S)

27

(b) **Prayer at Start of Meeting**

Lord of all life, we thank you for all the living opportunities of this new day; Lord of all truth, we ask you to open our minds to all that is waiting for us to know today; Lord of all compassion, we look to you for forgiveness for all we have done amiss, and for encouragement to be bold in sharing your compassion for all with whom we have to do. Through Jesus Christ our Lord. Amen.

(D W D S)

28

(c) **Prayer at Start of Meeting**

O Lord our God, who hast given us in the course of our duties to judge the achievements of others, in all our judgements grant us faithfulness to the truth as it is given us to know, and humility to prefer the welfare of others to the vindication of ourselves, that we may be inspired by the love of Christ by which we ourselves are judged, to which we are called, for we ask it in his name. Amen.

(D W D S)

29

(a) **Prayer at Start of Kirk Session**

O God, to whom we look for freedom and for truth, liberate us, we pray, from everything that keeps us from the truth, from wishful thinking and careless speaking, from entrenched positions and closed minds, from innuendo and destructive argument. In our deliberations this day give us the freedom to listen without prejudice and, it may be, to change our minds, that our aim may be the welfare of the congregation and parish we serve, and our judgements may be imaginative, informed, courageous and fair. Amen.

(D W D S)

30

(b) **Prayer at Start of Kirk Session**

O God, in whom are united beauty and goodness, justice and truth, grant that what we do this day may help and not hinder the coming of these things among us. Give us in our thinking, clarity, in our listening, charity, in our speaking, brevity, that in our deciding we may above all respect the truth, and each other, and those whom we are here to serve. Amen.

(D W D S)

31

Grace before Meal

(*For use with a Climbing Club*)

For the beauty which we have known in the high and lonely places,
    For the comradeship which we have found in difficult and dangerous places,
    For food and friendship which we now share,
    We give thanks. Amen.

(A W)

ERRATUM

It has been brought to the attention of the Publisher since publication that the following prayers have been printed without acknowledgment to the original source. This was due to an oversight for which we would like to extend our apologies to all concerned.

For Section I, Prayer 32, acknowledgment is due to *Contemporary Prayers for Public Worship*, Caryl Micklem (ed), SCM Press 1967, p 35.

For Section I, Prayers 49, 50, 58, Section II, Prayer 6, acknowledgment is due to *New Prayers for Worship*, Alan Gaunt.